Making the Grade

Meredith D. Gall, Ph.D.

in collaboration with

Joyce P. Gall, Ph.D.

Produced by M. Damien Publishers, Eugene, Oregon

Published by

 Prima Publishing and Communications
Post Office Box 1260MG
Rocklin, California 95677
(916) 624-5718

Copyright © 1988 by M. Damien Publishers

Produced by M. Damien Publishers, 4810 Mahalo Drive, Eugene, Oregon 97405; (503) 687-9055.

Published by Prima Publishing and Communications, Post Office Box 1260MG, Rocklin, California 95677-1260; (916) 624-5718.

Cover Design: The Dunlavey Studio, Sacramento, California
Illustrations: Judy Fairbairn
Composition: Editing & Design Services, Inc., Eugene, Oregon
Production Consultants: Bookmakers, Eugene, Oregon

Library of Congress Cataloging in Publication Data

Gall, Meredith D., 1942–
    Making the grade.

    Rev. ed. of: Study for success. © 1985.
    Includes index.
    Summary: Discusses eighty specific study techniques, relating them to such larger tasks as organizing for study, taking notes, writing papers, taking tests, and others.
    1. Study, Method of.   I. Gall, Joyce P.   II. Gall, Meredith D., 1942–   . Study for success.
III. Fairbairn, Judy.   IV. Title.
LB1049.G35 1988   371.3'028'12   88-9867

    ISBN 0-914629-74-3 (pbk.)

90 91 RRD 10 9 8 7 6 5 4 3 2

HOW TO ORDER: Quantity discounts are available from Prima Publishing & Communications, P.O. Box 1260MG, Rocklin, CA 95677; telephone (916) 624-5718. On your letterhead include information concerning the intended use of the books and the number of books you wish to purchase.

U.S. Bookstores and Libraries: Please submit all orders to St. Martin's Press, 175 Fifth Avenue, New York, NY 10010; telephone (212) 674-5151.

Manufactured in the United States of America.

Preface

Making the Grade is for students who have a sincere desire to do well in school. If you are such a student, this book will serve as your step-by-step guide toward greater academic success.

As you start applying the *Making the Grade* skills, you should see an improvement in your grades on assignments and tests. You will become better at figuring out what your instructor expects. You will also become more confident about your ability to learn. And you will cut down on wasted effort. You will learn how to study smarter, not harder.

Making the Grade presents 80 high-performance study skills. That may seem like a lot to learn, but really it is not. Each skill covers one small part of the overall study process. Thus, each skill is easily learned and put into practice. Also, many of the skills are interrelated. After you learn some initial skills, it is much easier to learn others.

You may find that you already know and use some of the skills. Reading about them in *Making the Grade* will build your confidence that you are on the right track. When you come to skills that are new to you, devote more attention to them. Select a few to work on. Read the section on each skill, and then practice it the first chance you get.

The 80 study skills apply to any school situation in which you are expected to study on your own. It does not matter whether you are in junior high or middle school, high school, college, or professional school. Whatever grade level or subject you are in, *Making the Grade* skills will work for you.

Take a minute now to look at the Table of Contents. You will see that the 80 skills are organized around five topics: getting started; taking notes and participating in class; reading textbooks; writing papers; and taking tests. These are the major tasks of study. The skills listed under each task give you the specific ways to perform that task effectively.

In reading this book, you will be taking an important step toward becoming a successful student. Every one of the 80 *Making the Grade* skills is effective. I learned some of the skills myself while in high school. I learned others as a student at Harvard and at the University of California, Berkeley. These skills worked for me and my classmates then, and they will work for you now.

In fact, you have an advantage over my classmates and me. We had to discover the skills slowly by trial and error. No book like *Making the Grade* was available to guide us. Also, I did not discover some of the skills until I became a university professor and started thinking about study from a professor's point of view. Finally, I discovered some of the skills from recent research about how good students learn.

As you learn the *Making the Grade* skills, you are bound to make an important discovery. Study skills are not only important to success in school. The same skills also are the key to success in whatever career or personal endeavor you choose. They will help you be a winner throughout life. The time to start learning them is now!

This book is written from the first author's perspective as a student and professor. It has also benefited greatly from the second author's contribution. Joyce was a fellow student of mine at Berkeley. She was thus able to add to my repertoire of study skills from her own experience as a student. In addition, she helped me to try out the first version of the book with students and to revise it subsequently.

Meredith D. Gall, Ph.D.
May 1988

Contents

6. Taking Tests *131*

1

Study Skills Pay Off

The purpose of this chapter is to sharpen your awareness of the importance of good study skills. If you improve your study skills, good things will happen — it will be easier to study, you will get better grades, and you will be more successful in life. These benefits of good study habits are explained below, as well as how you can use this book to improve your own study skills.

A Brief Personal Note

Recently I was asked where and how long I was a student. Well, I went to elementary school in California, high school in Connecticut, college in Massachusetts (Harvard University), and graduate school in California (the University of California, Berkeley). That's twenty years of school work!

Even though most of us are students for a long time, we seldom stop to think about how to be a *successful* student. I was a good student overall, but I had some bad study habits, and wasted a lot of time. I received failing or near failing grades in some of my courses. At those times I realized that I could not take high grades and test scores for granted.

Gradually I discovered the need to develop more *effective study skills*. But what are effective study skills, and how do you learn them? In my case, I had to learn many of the important study skills by myself, through trial and error. Fortunately, some of my classmates at Harvard and Berkeley told me the study methods that worked for them. I found their ideas very helpful.

Another source of insight into study skills has been my experience as a professor at the University of Oregon for the past nine years. I have learned how professors think and what they expect of students. This understanding is valuable, because "psyching out" the teacher is critical to success in school. If you know what the teacher expects, you will know what and how to study. More about this in the following chapters.

I have also learned how important it is to learn study skills early in your school career. Otherwise a big gap between your study skills and school requirements can develop. For example, consider Skill 60: Type your paper neatly on good paper. High school teachers do not usually require students to turn in typewritten papers. In college, however, many professors will only accept typewritten papers. And in graduate school, I do not know a single professor who accepts a paper that is not typed.

Clearly it pays to learn how to type while you are still in high school, or as soon as you start college. Some of my classmates avoided learning this skill. They ran into increasing difficulties during their school years. They were always worrying about whether their grade would be lowered. Some of my classmates hired a typist, but this was expensive and time consuming. I am glad that I learned to type during my second year of high school.

It took me a very long time to learn the study skills that lead to success in school and college. But you can take a shortcut. This book summarizes in one place all the essential skills for successful study. If you learn these skills, you will be successful in high school, college, and beyond. Why not put them to work for you now?

Can You Become a Better Student?

Yes, you can become a better student. Unfortunately, however, most people get fixed on a certain image of themselves as students early in life. They come to think of themselves as smart or stupid or average. Most students do not realize that they can become smarter if they learn study skills.

Why do so few students learn these skills? One reason is that teachers have many students to teach. They do not have time to work with each student on a one-to-one basis. Even if a student wants help on improving his or her study skills, it is often unavailable.

Another reason why students do not learn study skills is that teachers concentrate mostly on subject matter. They see themselves as teachers of math, history, biology, geography, and so forth. They do not see themselves as teachers of study skills.

Students could help each other learn study skills but they are not likely to do this. The reason is that schools are highly competitive. For example, I read recently that at Stanford University there were 12,500 applicants for 1,500 openings in the freshman class. When I went to graduate school at Berkeley, I was told that there were 100 applicants for each opening in the doctoral program.

Probably the best-known example of competition is pre-med courses. These courses are offered in college and are required for admission to medical school. The courses are usually graded "on the curve" so that only a certain percentage of students can get A's and B's. As a result, many students feel that they are cutting their own throats if they help someone else study for the course. The reasoning is that the worse other students do, the better they do.

Busy teachers, lack of instruction on study skills, and competition for grades: all these factors mean that you are on your own. Without help, you are stuck with your present level of study skills. With help, though, your study skills can improve dramatically. This book is ready to help you if you are ready to become a better student.

How the Book Is Organized and Who It Is For

Eighty study skills are presented in this book. All of them work toward a single purpose —to turn you into a successful learner who gets good grades. With effort on your part and use of this book, you can become a much better student than you now are.

Any student can profit from these study skills. If you are doing poorly in school right now, these skills will give you the basics — a place to start on the road to improvement. If you are an average student, you probably know some of the basic study skills presented here, but you can work on using them more regularly. You also will find many new study skills that you can start using.

Even if you are a superior student, there is much that you can learn here. The danger in being a superior student is that schoolwork is easy for you. Your study skills serve you well. However, even a superior student sometimes has difficulty in a course. When this happens, the student will need to learn new study skills or use existing skills more effectively. Also, a superior student may earn top grades in one school setting using particular study skills. In a new school setting, though, the competition can increase. This book shows you study skills that will help you through any competitive, difficult course you might take.

The study skills in this book are for students at any level. It does not matter whether you are in junior high school or middle school, in high school, college, or professional school. The same skills apply. For this reason it is important to learn these skills as soon as you can — certainly no later than high school. That way you can keep practicing and refining your study skills so that you will become more and more successful as you go through school.

I remember well my first year at Harvard. Students who had gone to private high schools like myself generally got better grades than students who went to public high schools. The reason is that the private school graduates were quite accustomed to competitive, difficult study. They could meet the demands of Harvard. Public school graduates had not been similarly challenged and so they had a lot of catching up to do. Most of them caught up by their second or third year of college, but they were operating at a disadvantage until then.

The study skills in this book apply to any subject. For example, the basic process of studying computer science is not different from the basic process of studying literature or economics. No matter what course you take, you are probably going to attend class, read textbooks, and take tests. If you know how to take a test in computer science, you will know how to take a test in literature or any other subject.

The book is organized in terms of the study tasks that are expected of you in most courses. There are separate chapters on writing course papers, taking tests, taking notes in class and participating in discussions, and reading textbooks. There is also an important chapter on getting a study session started. If you can overcome procrastination, you are well along the way to becoming a superior student.

The book provides clear descriptions of study skills that work. I have used each of these skills and have observed other successful students use them.

Why Study Skills Are Important

It used to be that graduating from college — any college — was sufficient to ensure a good job or admission to graduate school. This is no longer true. Now you need to graduate *with good grades* from a good college. And to get admitted to a good college, you need to earn superior grades in high school and do well on college entrance tests. And how do you do this? By using effective study skills.

In other words, you need to start using good study skills *before* you get to college if you want to be successful in college and later in life.

Study is crucial to success in school, but more study is not necessarily better than less study. Quality of study is what counts. A researcher found recently that students who hit the books for 20 to 30 hours weekly — but who engaged in high-quality efforts — did as well as students who spent many more hours in lower-quality study. This book supports these research findings. I am not arguing that you should study harder, just *smarter*.

Is it really worth it to learn the study skills for writing term papers, taking notes, and preparing for exams? The answer is, yes. As I stated above, study skills will help you get good grades in school. Furthermore, study skills will be useful throughout your life. Study skills involve planning, organizing your time, setting goals, solving problems, tracking down information, and communicating ideas. These skills are equally important for success in professional work. The systematic, well-organized, achieving student becomes the systematic, well-organized, achieving adult.

Finding the Motivation to Study

Even if you have good study skills, you will not use them unless you are motivated. If you lack a purpose for going to school, if your school environment is unpleasant, if you hate your courses — you will have little energy for serious study.

I think that motivation for study is influenced by four factors. Your decision concerning each factor will greatly affect how much energy you are willing to invest in your studies. The examples below refer to college but my points apply equally to high school and to graduate school.

1. *Life goals.* What do you want from life? What are your goals? A recent survey found that today's college freshmen have these career goals: being well-off financially, obtaining recognition from colleagues and peers, and having administrative responsibility for the work of others. Are these your goals, too? You need not have these particular goals, but it does matter that you have goals.

It is also important to determine whether school is important to the achievement of your goals. For example, college will not make sense to you unless it relates to your personal goals. If college makes no sense, then you will be unmotivated to study effectively.

If you are unclear about your goals, what can you do? There are many paths you can take — talking to parents and friends, reading books, personal reflection. Another approach that can be helpful is to talk to a school or career counselor. These professionals are expert at helping people define and clarify their goals.

2. *Choice of school.* If college makes sense to you, you will need to submit applications for admission. This can be a difficult problem because there are thousands of higher education institutions in this country. There are junior colleges, colleges, universities, and specialized professional schools. These institutions are

public or private, secular or religious. Some are expensive, others are low-cost. You might be happy at one school and miserable at another.

It is important to select a school that is right for you. If you are happy with your school, you will be more motivated to study effectively. There are several ways to find out about the characteristics of different schools. Directories of colleges are available. Your school counselors are also a good source of information, as are people who have graduated from various colleges.

3. *Choice of college major.* After being admitted to college, you have another big decision to make. You will need to select a "major," which is a program of studies in a discipline. You can select from among the traditional disciplines such as history, English, sociology, chemistry, and economics. Or at some colleges and universities you can make up your own major, usually in an interdisciplinary subject such as minority studies, women's studies, or the cinema.

It is important to realize that some colleges may not offer the major that interests you. At Harvard, for example, undergraduates cannot major in business, but many other universities offer an undergraduate major in this field. California universities do not offer an undergraduate major in education, but universities in many other states do so. Universities, being large institutions, have the advantage that they can offer more majors — and more courses in each major — than a typical college.

How do you select a college major? There are a few obvious considerations. Most important is your personal and career interests. If you do not have a deep interest in your major, you will not be motivated to study for the required courses.

The other important consideration in selecting a college major is your talents and abilities. You may be interested in economics but find that you have no talent for it. Some subjects fascinate me — like architecture and astronomy — but I would make a poor architect or astronomer. This is because I lack some of the abilities needed to be a success in these fields. Even if I studied very hard, I would have difficulty competing against students with better natural abilities in these areas.

Obviously you should select a college major that matches your interests and talents. Career counselors can help you do this. They can give you vocational interest tests to help determine your interest patterns objectively. Also, they can give you aptitude tests to determine whether you have the abilities — verbal, quantitative, musical, etc. — that are emphasized in certain college majors. The task of studying will be much simpler and more enjoyable if you select a college major that matches your talents and interests.

4. *Financing your education.* I have known many students who have financed their education by working and attending school at the same time. My advice is this: try to arrange your finances so that you can attend school full time and not work at all. The most I ever worked at Harvard was five hours a week.

If you must work, I recommend you do it full time during summers and vacation periods when you are not enrolled in school. If you try to work and study at the same time, you risk doing neither well. Another alternative is to take a reduced courseload so that you can work part time. The drawback, though, is that you lengthen the amount of time required to get your degree. It is better to get loans and live simply so that you can finish school as soon as possible. Once you have finished school, your earning power is much greater than with the kinds of jobs you can get as a student. In other words, you can finance your education better *after* you have finished school than while you are in school.

How to Study this Book

One way to study this book would be to read it from cover to cover, taking notes along the way. This is an ineffective study method. I recommend instead that you get an idea of what the book is about by examining the list of skills at the front of the book. Next, select a chapter that describes a study task that concerns you. Read it and select a few study skills (no more than three or four) to try out. Practice using these skills until you feel comfortable with them. Then select some additional skills to master from the same chapter, or skip to skills presented in another chapter.

The above method puts you in the position of being an *active* learner. Instead of being a passive reader, you will read actively and make use of what you have read. This is the essence of effective study.

If you use the study skills as indicated, you should see results right away. Each study session will become more productive. Your feelings of success will motivate you to keep using the skills. Some skills are harder than others to master, though. Practice is the only solution to this problem. I recall my efforts to learn the game of racquetball a few years ago. Some of the skills came quickly to me, but others — like serving the ball and hitting Z-shots — took much longer to master. I could not ignore these difficult skills. Each of them is essential to racquetball. I just needed to keep practicing and be satisfied with slow, gradual improvement.

School Terminology

I use some words in this book that may not be familiar to you. I will explain them here.

After kindergarten and elementary school, a student goes to junior high school (usually grades 7-8 or 7-9). Nowadays some cities have middle schools (grades 6-8) instead. After high school (usually grades 9-12), you may decide to go to college.

College requires four years of study. The only differences between a college and a *university* are that a university is often larger and includes a graduate school. Some students go to a *community college* (sometimes called a junior college), where they can complete up to two years of college study.

College usually consists of required courses and courses in your major. A *college major* is the subject which you have chosen as your area of specialization. You can major in engineering, English, mathematics, physics, or one of many other subjects.

When you graduate from college, you receive a *bachelor's degree*. This degree is usually called a "B.A." or "B.S."

depending on whether you receive a bachelor of arts degree or a bachelor of science degree.

If you decide to keep studying after college, you will go to a *graduate school*. Graduate schools are usually part of universities. There you can study to be a doctor, lawyer, philosopher, scientist, teacher, or other type of professional. Study in graduate school is usually called *graduate work,* whereas college study is called *undergraduate work*. When you complete your graduate work, you will receive an M.A. (master of arts), Ph.D. (doctor of philosophy), MBA (master of business administration), J.D. (doctor of jurisprudence), M.D. (doctor of medicine), or other degree depending upon your program of study.

2

Getting Started

The hardest part of being a student is getting yourself to hit the books. There were many times that my classmates and I would say something like, "If I could just get started on this paper ..." Students can think of many ways to delay studying — lingering over dinner, watching TV, playing a computer game, talking on the phone — *anything* seems more appetizing than the prospect of sitting at a desk to study. The problem can become so disabling that it results in poor grades in high school or failure in college. I am therefore devoting an entire chapter to solutions for this problem.

The process of delaying or putting off a task is called *procrastination*. I know three reasons why procrastination is so common among students. First, school requires a lot of self-motivation. No one is looking over your shoulder telling you first to do this, then that. You are very much on your own. True, the teacher may tell you what to read and write, and when assignments are due. But the teacher cannot follow you around constantly to make certain that you get the work done.

College and graduate school put even more responsibilities on your shoulders than junior high and high school do. Relatively little guidance of your learning is provided. Original research is a requirement. Thus, there is a premium on self-motivation. If you want to succeed in college or graduate school, it helps greatly to be a self-starter.

Since no one can force you to work, it is easy to avoid attending classes, studying textbooks, writing term papers, and so on. A similar situation is found in the world of work. I have observed that if employees are not supervised, some of them will work as little as possible. They may take long lunches, gossip with their workmates, wander off. These activities are seen as preferable to work. For this reason business and industry make use of time clocks, supervisors, inspectors, and production quotas. These devices keep people on-task and motivated. Unfortunately, the workers are negatively motivated rather than positively motivated.

To summarize, one reason why many students procrastinate is that they lack self-motivation. To put it another way, there is no one around to make them study.

The second reason for procrastination is that so much of school work is unstructured. Even if you wish to study, you may be unsure about how to proceed. For example, the teacher's directions for a paper may be something as vague as, "Write a 10-page paper comparing the governments of Canada and the United States." That is not much to go on. Where do you start? What sequence of steps should you follow? What should you put in the paper? What books and research studies should you cite? The task is so unstructured that you hesitate to start. Thus are the seeds of procrastination sown.

The third reason for procrastination is that study is sometimes very difficult. You cannot always take easy courses. If you are planning to go to college, you may be required to take courses that are difficult for you. I find myself in similar situations, even though it has been many years since I finished going to school. My job — and this is true of most people's jobs — requires that I continue learning new skills. Some of this learning comes easily because I already know a lot about my specialty, but some of it is quite difficult. When I need to study these difficult topics, I feel the desire to procrastinate. Virtually anything seems more pleasant than the frustration of studying something complex and unclear.

Mild forms of procrastination are tolerable. We may put off a difficult or unstructured study task for a few days, but finally we get down to brass tacks. Unfortunately, procrastination may have more serious consequences. I recall college students who procrastinated so much that they fell hopelessly behind in their homework. These students had no option but to drop out of school for the remainder of the term or academic year. When they resumed their studies, they had to retake the same courses they failed to finish.

One of the worst consequences of procrastination is that it robs you of the pleasure that you would otherwise experience in your leisure time. As you watch TV, chat with your friends, play cards, or whatever, your conscience keeps telling you, "I should be studying." You start worrying that you cannot seem to get down to work. The worrying can worsen to the point that worry itself becomes a source of procrastination. Every minute you spend in worry is a minute away from your studies.

Now I ask you to consider some relatively simple skills that can help you break out of the procrastination trap. Most of these skills are intended to help you get your study sessions started. Once you get started — reading the first page of a textbook assignment, making a few notes for a school paper — you will generate enough momentum to keep going.

Skill 1.   *Spend some time on study each day so work does not pile up.*

One of the worst things a student can do is to let work pile up. The bigger the pile, the harder it is to make a dent in it. Avoid at all cost getting behind in your studies. In practice, this means that you should allocate some time to study almost every day. It need not be for a long period of time. An hour or two each day may be sufficient.

When I was a student, I tried to study six days a week. I reserved one day a week to let my mind rest completely. (At most I would reserve two days a week for this purpose.) Another thing I did was to spend some time each day on *each* of my courses. This meant, on some days, that I spent several hours on an assignment requiring immediate attention, and just a few minutes mentally reviewing where I stood in each of my other courses. (More about this technique when I discuss Skill 3.)

I sometimes departed from this strategy but regretted it later. The worst experience occurred my first year at Harvard. Foreign languages were never my strong suit, but it was a university requirement that I take a course in this subject. I chose Introductory German, and the professor said that he would emphasize teaching us how to speak German and to translate spoken German.

I started going to the German language lab but was quickly frustrated because I could not distinguish some of the sounds and words on the training tapes. The labs became so aversive that I put off going to them. Going to class also became a painful experience because I could not respond when the professor called on me. Naturally I got further and further behind in the course. I knew I should resume going to the labs, but could not bring myself to do so. A victim of procrastination, I had let so many lessons go unstudied that it seemed impossible to ever catch up.

Finally, in an act born of desperation, fear, and sheer will power, I made a marathon effort to study for the final exam. I received a C- for the course, not a good grade for a student on full scholarship.

The obvious solution to having work pile up is to study every day. The amount of time you spend is less important than a schedule of regular, daily study. If you procrastinate for more than a few days, you need to analyze the situation and take immediate corrective action. The next skills in this chapter are some of these "corrective actions."

Skill 2.   When given a study assignment, do some work on it right away.

Time management experts recommend that you take immediate action on any assigned task. It does not matter how simple or complex the task is. Act immediately on it if you can.

This principle is widely applied in business and industry. Executives are trained never to let a piece of paper cross their desk twice. This practice makes sense when you realize that people waste time if they read a letter or memo and then put it aside in a

"To Do" file. They later have to pull the letter or memo from the file and re-read it, which is wasted time. Also, an executive may discover that certain preliminary steps need to be completed, such as tracking down background information, before the main action can be taken. These steps could have been done right away by a secretary during the time that the memo was sitting in the executive's "To Do" file. Procrastination breeds inefficiency.

Another example of the payoff from taking immediate action comes from a prominent executive, who also was a state senator. She told me that her most difficult task was giving speeches at various functions. I asked her how she prepared her speeches. She replied that upon receiving an invitation to speak, she immediately made a few notes about what to say. The next day she would examine her notes, make changes, and elaborate on the points she wanted to make. During free moments, too, she thought about the speech, and if ideas came to her, she jotted them down. Within a period of four or five days, she usually had a complete outline of the speech.

If she did not go through this process, she said, the speech would haunt her. When she finally would sit down to prepare it, few ideas came to mind. This busy executive learned the hard way that it was essential for her to act immediately after accepting a speech invitation.

The practice of taking immediate action on a newly assigned task is easily applied to school study. Suppose you are asked near the start of the term to write a paper that will be due at the end of the term. The choice of topic is up to you. Your first response might be, "Well, it's early yet. I have a few weeks before I have to worry about this particular project." A better response might be, "The first thing I need to do is decide on a topic. I'll take a few minutes now to get a binder page and start listing possible ideas for a topic. Then every few days I'll review my list, scratch out topics I no longer wish to consider, and add new topics."

This better response follows the principle of taking immediate action, even if the action is minimal. In this way you avoid delaying to the point that the term paper becomes a thorn in your side.

Reading assignments also benefit from the *Principle of Immediate Action*. A teacher will usually give you a reading list for his or her course at the beginning of the term. Your "immediate action" might be to review the reading list, due dates, whereabouts of each book, and total amount of reading required. Next you can put together a schedule: how much reading do you have to do each day in order to finish on time? Although these actions only take a few minutes, they get the ball rolling. You become actively involved with the reading list.

Some students advocate a strategy that is exactly the opposite of what I recommend. They think that reading assignments should be put off until they have sat through most of the teacher's class sessions. Their reasoning is that when they finally get around to doing the reading assignments, they will understand them better because they now have the benefit of the teacher's wisdom.

I agree that it helps to have advance knowledge about a subject prior to reading or writing about it. However, I believe it is a better strategy to start reading or writing as soon as possible. Then revise your writing or review what you have read when your understanding of the subject deepens. The same strategy is used in R & D (research and development) programs of business and industry: make a rough version of the product, try it out, revise it based on what you have learned, and continue testing and revising until the goal is achieved. Similarly, reading-and-revising or writing-and-reviewing is generally more effective than a one-shot effort.

Skill 3.   *Maintain continuity of study, so you do not lose the thread.*

I find it maddening to start work on a project and then leave it for a period of time. When I return to the project, I have completely forgotten where I was on it. Many times I made a partial draft of a paper, and then was interrupted from completing it by other tasks having higher priority. When I returned to the paper, I usually had forgotten what I was writing about and how far the paper was toward completion. I may even have misplaced some of my notes and reference books. Furthermore, everything had turned "cold." Even though the partial draft was my own writing, it looked unfamiliar to me. It usually took several hours for me to catch up to the point where I left off a writing project. Worst of all, I delayed catching up because I kept thinking about the mess awaiting me.

The solution to this problem is obvious. Once you have started a study project, keep working on it. This does not mean that you should spend an equal amount of time on the project each day. It does mean you should spend *some* time each day. Occasionally I will take a day or two off, but any interruption that lasts more than two or three days is likely to break my train of thought.

If you must leave a study project for more than several days, make a note about where you are leaving it. For example, if you are in the process of reading a textbook, write down the page on which you stopped reading, and make sure your note pages are labeled with the name of the book so you know what they refer to. Then make certain you store everything where it can be easily retrieved. Careful labeling and storage will avoid the problem of having your study projects go "cold" on you due to interruptions.

Skill 4.   Break a big task into small, manageable tasks.

I probably use this skill more than any other skill described in this book.

This is the eighth book that I have written or co-authored. Friends and colleagues wonder how I can be so productive. They say, "I don't think I could bring myself to write just one book. Where do you start? How do you get organized? How do you write page after page?" I respond to these questions by saying that I break down what seems like an impossibly large task — writing a book — into many small tasks. I point out that if you write one page a day, you will write a 365-page book in a year. Figure that revising and refining your book can be done at the rate of two pages a day, which totals 183 days (half a year). Allow another half year for library research and other forms of information collection. In a period of two years, then, spending no more than an hour or two a day, you can write a substantial book. The trick is to break the large, overwhelming task into small, manageable ones.

I wrote my first book this way. Every day, after working at the office and having dinner, I would take a short nap to rest and to clear my head. Then I worked for two hours on the book. Some nights I would use my time quota to do library research. When I had collected enough material, I used my time quota to write. After spending two hours on book writing, I still had plenty of time to watch TV, read, or whatever.

The *first* step in using this skill is to analyze a large assignment into many small tasks. Each task should be accomplishable within a single study session. Suppose the assignment is to read and study a textbook of approximately 500 pages. You are allowed the entire semester to complete the assignment. Looking at the textbook, you figure you can read five pages in an hour, which is all the time you want to spend. You also figure that it is no bother to spend 15 minutes reviewing parts of the textbook that you have previously read.

After breaking the large assignment into small tasks, the *second* step is to make each small task a goal for a study session. For example, you can tell yourself, "Today I will read five pages and spend 15 minutes reviewing Chapter 4." When you complete the task, give yourself a pat on the back. If you can tolerate more, define an additional small task and accomplish it. If you find that you were too ambitious in defining a task, revise downward what you intend to accomplish the next day. Be sure not to define tasks that you cannot finish. Your lack of success will discourage you. Once in this state of mind, you are likely to avoid getting back to the assignment for days on end.

The skill of breaking a large task into small, manageable tasks really works. I used it throughout junior high school, high school, college and graduate school. I continue to use it in my professional career. The skill also helps one to accomplish personal goals. For example, several years ago a friend got me interested in body building. In my zeal I developed a program of exercises that required a two-hour workout to complete. I was exhausted at the end of these sessions. Eventually I neglected going to the gym because I did not want to face such demanding workouts. My body-building program went up in smoke.

When I finally realized what was happening, I analyzed all the exercises in my weightlifting program. I was trying to accomplish too much in one workout (just as one can try to accomplish too much in one study session). The solution was to separate my exercises into separate workouts, each one requiring less than an hour to complete. Yes, it does require more trips to the gym, but the fact is that I am actually doing my workouts. Indeed, I look forward to them because they produce physical and psychological benefits without wearing me out in the process.

Skill 5.   Set minimal goals for each study session.

The practice of setting minimal goals was mentioned in describing Skill 4. It is so important, though, that I want to present it as a separate skill.

Once you have broken down a large assignment into a number of small tasks, you must decide how much to accomplish in each study session. Like some students, I used to set unrealistically high study goals for myself. I achieved my objective sometimes, but more often I would fall short. In fact, on more than one occasion I set a high goal for a study session, and then promptly found something else to do — like shoot pool, see a movie, or play bridge.

I have learned over the years that the opposite strategy — setting easy goals for each study session — is more effective. Just set an easy goal if you feel resistance to studying. For example, I might tell myself, "Today I'll just study for an hour." On occasion I have even set a time goal of a half hour. If a time goal is not appropriate, then set another type of study goal — for example, reading five pages in a textbook, or making a half-page outline of a term paper, or doing a set of ten math problems. If you set a goal but still hesitate to get started, set the goal even lower.

The technique of setting minimal goals is powerful. It should help you overcome most study blocks.

Skill 6.   Set reasonable standards for your initial efforts on an assignment.

Most students have no reluctance about writing a personal letter to a good friend or about talking on the phone. The same students will get anxious and delay writing a school paper or preparing a class presentation. Why is this?

The main reason for the lack of anxiety and delay in the personal situations is that our standards of performance are not demanding. We do what comes naturally. We do not worry about our grammar, spelling, or eloquence. In school situations our standards are likely to be much higher. We know that our work will be evaluated by the teacher, probably in comparison with the work of other students. We also know that our work must follow strict rules of grammar, style, and logic. No wonder we put off studying.

In short, anxiety about high standards and "rules" is a source of procrastination. A good way to deal with this anxiety is to ignore standards and rules for a while. Conduct your studies in a natural, easy manner.

What does this mean in practice? Suppose you need to prepare a class presentation on a topic. You want it to be good because the teacher and your classmates will be listening to your efforts. Rather than getting freaked out by this assignment, I suggest you make a few rough notes. Just get your thoughts on paper without worrying about quality. Then talk naturally from your notes into a tape recorder.

This procedure will give you a good start on the assignment. As you listen to the recording, you can fill out your notes and decide whether you need to research the topic further. At this point you can begin thinking about standards and rules. You are over the initial hurdle of getting started on the assignment. After further work, you can make another tape recording and decide whether you are ready to give the presentation or whether additional revision is necessary. This method of reaching a goal through approximations is very effective.

One further note about the technique of avoiding high standards for initial study efforts. Bright students tend to procrastinate because they set extremely high standards for themselves. If you are such a student, it helps to realize that you are feeling the pressure of high expectations. You can get this pressure off your back by doing a first version of an assignment without worrying about its quality.

Skill 7.   *Do something pleasurable after a study session, not before.*

Rewards are extremely important to the maintenance of your study behavior. Study is hard work and you deserve to be rewarded for it —*now*. Without immediate rewards for studying, you will be increasingly reluctant to put in the necessary effort. Unfortunately, the real rewards of study are usually far removed in the future. If you study hard and do well in school, you may be rewarded some day with a satisfying professional job, stereo equipment, a sporty car, prestige, financial ability to raise a family, and so on. It is difficult, though, to see the connection between your study efforts on a Monday evening and these rewards.

What kinds of immediate rewards can you build into your daily schedule? The rewards should be readily available, brief, and inexpensive. When I was in college my "immediate rewards" consisted of such activities as having a late-night snack at a favorite hangout with a friend, seeing a movie if I finished my studies early in the evening, shooting pool, or engaging in pleasure reading. Your own rewards may be different, but that is not important. What is important is planning activities that you genuinely enjoy.

A big mistake made by some students is to engage in pleasant activities *before* they begin to study. They may plan to watch a favorite TV program, call a friend, have a snack, and then study. By this time their motivation is gone. Study seems unpleasurable compared to these other activities. Therefore you should analyze which of them can be deferred until after you have completed a study session. Remember: study first, indulge later. As you study you can think about the fun that lies ahead.

A good technique is to build mini-rewards into a study session. The end of a study session is not soon enough for me to get a reward, so every half hour or so I take a brief break of five to ten minutes. I may get a bite to eat, make a quick phone call, read an article in a news magazine, or check out the TV schedule. Even getting out of my chair for a few minutes is pleasurable. These mini-rewards often help me maintain an extended study session of several hours or more.

Another effective way to get immediate rewards is to have something pleasant accompany your study session. For example, I listen to background music while I am reading or thinking. When I write, I sometimes keep the TV on, with the volume turned low. As long as the background music or TV is not distracting, I find it helps to extend the length of my study sessions. (For the same reason music is piped into buildings to keep workers or shoppers in a pleasant, energetic mood.)

Some people say that it is bad to study for external rewards such as going to the movies or for a snack. Study should be pursued, they claim, for its *intrinsic* rewards. In other words, study should be its own reward. This argument has some merit. Books do contain exciting ideas, and writing a school essay can be very satisfying. However, the truth is that most of us need both intrinsic and external rewards. For example, if we have the right sort of job, we enjoy our work activities for their own sake. But it is also nice to receive a paycheck at the end of the month so that we can buy the necessities of life and some fun items.

I am of the opinion that many people study initially for external rewards. Later study becomes a source of intrinsic rewards as people discover that they are learning exciting new ideas. The reverse can also happen. Some people start studying a subject because they are intrinsically excited about it. Eventually their intrinsic interest develops into a career, which then produces external rewards.

In summary, intrinsic and external rewards are not mutually exclusive. They can work together to motivate your studies.

Skill 8.   If you get stuck on an assignment, see a teacher, classmate, or tutor.

You may put off your studies simply because you do not know what to do. For example, my classmates and I were sometimes unable to do problem sets in mathematics because they were so difficult. Even though I had allotted sufficient time to study, I could not use it productively because I was stuck.

My doctoral courses in statistics were especially difficult. Our textbook was confusing, and the professor's lectures were of no help. When it came time to solve the problems at the end of a textbook chapter, most of us did not know what to do. Our textbook and lecture notes were of little help.

What do you do in this situation? Some students got demoralized and failed the course. They left the university eventually, because a passing grade in statistics is required for advancement toward the doctorate. Others of us were more succesful. Rather than ignoring the problem, we decided to pool our wits. We formed study groups, which met regularly to discuss the assigned problem sets. Our meetings were very productive. They kept us working rather than procrastinating. Also, we were able to provide moral support for each other. And by bouncing ideas off each other, we did manage to solve most of the problems.

If you are stuck on your homework, a study group may be the solution. (I do not know of any teachers who object to study groups.) There are other ways to get help, too. You can ask another student for assistance. Or you can ask the teacher for help after class. Still another option is to find a tutor in your subject field. Some colleges and universities have a service that matches students with qualified tutors. If such a service is not available, you will need to search on your own for a tutor. Some tutors advertise their availability in student newspapers and on hallway bulletin boards.

I highly recommend the use of a tutor if you are having a difficult time in a course, especially a course that is in your major area of study. The neat feature of tutoring is that it is a one-to-one situation. Thus, it is entirely individualized in terms of your needs and learning style. Also, tutoring is nonthreatening. You can ask any question you wish, and you can target the tutor's assistance to aspects of the subject that most confuse you. Even if you have to pay the tutor an hourly fee, it is worth it. Which is more costly in the long run: getting a low or failing grade in a crucial course, or the cost of a tutor? If the tutor can help you get past a learning block, he or she is well worth the cost.

Study blocks can occur in any subject. I recall from my Harvard days that there was a small group of undergraduates who had great difficulty learning foreign languages. These students were at a loss because they could not receive a degree from Harvard unless they earned a satisfactory grade in their foreign language courses or on proficiency exams. Oddly enough, these students generally were very bright in other subject areas. Some of them were considered gifted. But they were simply unable to speak or translate a foreign language.

Harvard students who had this problem were assigned special tutors. This usually worked. The tutors were able to help most of them overcome their handicap so that they could satisfy the foreign language requirement. I heard about a few cases where, after every method was tried and failed, the foreign language requirement was waived.

In summary, if you are completely stuck on a homework assignment, try not to get down about it. And do not procrastinate. Get assistance from someone — your teacher, another student, a study group, or a tutor. Most learning blocks can be overcome.

Skill 9.   Schedule study sessions when you feel energy peaks.

I experience a variety of energy levels during a typical day. I feel mentally alert in the evening, from 8:00 on. At mid-morning and around 5:00 in the afternoon, I have a feeling of fatigue that is hard to shake. Other people have different patterns of alertness and fatigue, but we all tend to fluctuate up and down during each day.

I take advantage of these energy fluctuations by doing most of my serious professional study in the evening. During the day I generally do routine chores that do not place a burden on my thinking and creative capabilities.

Similarly, I advise you to analyze your patterns of mental energy and fatigue. Schedule your periods of study when your energy level is on an upswing. Take your study breaks, or do necessary study tasks which are not taxing mentally, at points when your energy is low.

If I do feel tired before sitting down to study (sometimes the thought of study is sufficient to tire me), I will take a few minutes to brew a cup of tea. Some of you may prefer coffee or soda or an energy snack such as raisins or trail mix. Many years ago I occasionally took No-Doz (a non-prescription drug to keep alert), but I stopped because of concern about possible side effects. The act of making a cup of tea seems to concentrate my attention. And the tea itself has enough caffeine to pep me up so that I feel motivated to study.

Skill 10. Use relaxation techniques and exercise to put yourself in a positive mood for study.

I am easily distracted and also get tense under stress. When this happens, it is difficult for me to study. My attention wanders from one thing to another, or I worry about things that happened during the day.

These problems used to waste a great deal of my time. One technique I learned for solving them was to relax before studying. Basically all I do is to instruct myself to calm down. I lie or sit down, close my eyes, and concentrate on my breathing until I am conscious of my inhaling and exhaling. When I feel that I am calm and relaxed, I start my study session.

My relaxation method also includes elements of meditation. Concentrating on one's breathing is a form of meditation. I also try to clear my mind so that it is free of all thoughts. It is important, however, not to worry about thoughts that do come into your mind. If you start worrying about the fact that you cannot keep your mind clear, you defeat the whole purpose of meditation. Just let the thoughts come and go without focusing on them.

Relaxation and meditation techniques are very effective. They are increasingly recommended by physicians, psychologists, and others. In fact, these techniques are used by some businessmen to increase their productivity and that of their employees. Excellent, brief books are available to help you become acquainted with meditation and relaxation methods. I have listed a few of them at the end of the chapter. Also, some colleges, universities, and clinics offer workshops that will train you systematically in these methods.

Another of my problems is hyperactivity. This means that I am easily distracted, have a short attention span, and get fidgety. Hyperactivity is usually a male problem. In school-age children hyperactivity is 17 times more prevalent among boys than among girls. My problem is not severe, but I do have difficulty sitting in a chair for more than half an hour at a time. In contrast, most female students whom I have observed are able to remain in their chairs studying for hours at a time.

To deal with this problem, I find it very helpful to engage in vigorous physical activity. Whenever I feel jumpy and at loose ends, I try to find a sport to play. I used to play a lot of squash (similar to racquetball) at Harvard. After several games of squash and a shower, I usually felt calm and ready to study. Nowadays I play racquetball, jog, and lift weights to get the same effect. Interestingly, these physical activities do not tire me. The effect is just the opposite: they increase my reserves of mental energy. This may have something to do with the fact that exercise increases the flow of oxygen to the brain.

Skill 11. Keep your study materials accessible and organized.

If your study area gets to be a mess, you will tend to avoid it. It is aggravating to have books and papers scattered all over so that you cannot easily locate what you need. There have been times when my desk looked organized and neat, yet all sorts of things were missing or hard to get my hands on. I avoided going near my study area then.

It is important to realize that organizing your study area is a continuous chore. You must allot time for this purpose. For example, I spent an hour today sorting out a great mass of material that I had thrown into a stack during the preceding school year. I organized the stuff into five categories: professional reading to be done; background material for future reference; material to file; things to take action on; and stuff to throw out. I still have a lot of work to do, but at least now I have a sense of where to start.

In addition to allotting time, you can take other steps to maintain the accessibility of your study materials. I recommend getting a large desk and several open shelves. Organize each of your study projects into a separate stack on your desk or on a shelf. In this way your various study projects will be in easy reach and visible.

The alternative is to put everything into a high stack or to shove it into drawers. The problem with this approach becomes apparent when you have to find things. You can waste a great deal of time weeding through a bunch of stuff just to locate the few things you need.

Another organizing technique is to clean house occasionally. Like many people, I have a tendency to collect things — the packrat syndrome. Term after term I used to pile up course textbooks, papers, teacher's handouts, lecture notes, copies of journal articles, homework assignments, correspondence. I became so swamped with the old material that I could not put my hands on what I needed *now*. The solution is to throw things out or give them away. It is hard to do, but you feel great after it is finished.

Here is an idea if you find it impossible to decide what to throw out. Tell yourself, "You can only keep half of what you have accumulated." This means that you have to sort out your priorities. It allows you to be a bit of a packrat, but keeps the impulse under control. I have used this technique often and found it very helpful.

Another good technique for cleaning house is to throw out anything that you have not looked at or used for the last year or two. The exception may be the few items that you wish to keep for sentimental reasons. Finally, remind yourself that your accumulation of school materials takes up a lot of room, and it requires a lot of effort to transport them when you change residence. Paper is heavy!

Another organizing technique is to label anything that is not clearly identifiable. Date everything; indicate what course it belongs to; put labels on your file folders. Also, create an index to your file cabinet if you have one. It is very annoying to search for a particular file folder inside a file cabinet. The files tend to be packed together, and the file labels are not easy to read unless you have hanging files. (A hanging file involves special file folders that fit on a metal suspension system.) An index, on the other hand, is easily searched and can be kept on your desk within easy reach. Also, the index can be used to describe where to place new materials in your file cabinet. For more on indexes, read the section on Skill 12.

In all the years that I have maintained a study area, I have never devised a perfect system for organizing my materials. A particular system will work for a while, but then it needs to be changed as my work projects change. Once you accept this as a fact of life, you can deal with it by allotting time occasionally for study organization. Otherwise your study area will become disorganized and no longer meet your needs.

Skill 12.   *Put loose papers in files, and create an index to them.*

I am a strong believer in using files to organize various papers. Business people and scholars alike use them extensively. You might as well learn how they can help you while you are still a student.

File folders and a two-drawer metal file cabinet are relatively cheap if you buy them on sale. You could buy a cardboard file cabinet, but they are less durable and not much cheaper than the metal kind. Also, you should buy "three-cut" file folders, which means that some of the label sections are positioned to the right side, some are positioned to the left, and some are in the middle. The three-cut feature makes it easier to find files in your cabinet. You can buy gummed labels (color-coded or plain) to put on the label section of the file folder, or you can write a description of the file's contents directly on the file folder.

I recommend that you buy "letter-size" folders and cabinets unless you are studying to be a lawyer, in which case the longer "legal-size" folders may be more appropriate. If you have the money to spend, you can buy a hanging file system to insert inside your cabinet. This system keeps your file folders from getting scrunched up next to each other, and makes it easier to pull a folder from the cabinet.

Your files will be much more accessible if you create an index to them. My index is on sheets of binder paper inserted in a three-ring binder. Most of my projects are in chronological order. I start a new page for each new year, and I number each study project consecutively within years. Each file folder is keyed to the index by putting the year and project number on the file folder label in this way: 1982-1, 1982-2, 1982-3, and so on. Table 1 provides an example of what such an index might look like.

Table 1. Example of an Index to One's Files

1982-1   Economics 315 (Macro-economics), Winter 1982

1982-2   International Relations 388, Winter 1982
      • lecture notes
      • term paper
      • handouts

1982-3   Tutorial with Professor Harrington, Winter 1982

1982-4   Tennis and other sports

1982-5   Mathematics 221 (probability), Spring 1982

1982-6   Economics 318 (decision theory), Spring 1982
      • lecture notes
      • homework assignments
      • final exam

1982-7   Psychology 300 (clinical and personality), Spring 1982

1982-8   Psychology 305 (field experience), Spring 1982

1982-9   Info about summer jobs and applications

Note that I have included some non-study activities (e.g., 1982-4) in the index too. Also note that some projects have several file folders (e.g., 1982-2), but I did not give them separate numbers.

All are given the same label. If you wish, though, you could dif-
ferentiate them in this way: 1982-2A, 1982-2B, and 1982-2C.

A chronological index is useful for any time-related event. If
you can remember the approximate year that an event occurred,
you can quickly turn to the appropriate binder page and see what
file or files you have on it.

Other kinds of material are best indexed under subject
headings. For example, you might create a "Personal" index
with such subject headings as Car, Insurance, Checking and Sav-
ings Account, Passport, and so forth. I also have a third index
for filing journal reprints and miscellaneous publications under
subject headings: Teaching Methods, Curriculum Development,
Study Skills, and so forth. File folders keyed to each of your indexes (chronologically-based projects, personal matters,
reference materials, etc.) should be kept in separate parts of your
file cabinet.

This filing system appears complex, but it is actually easy to
set up and operate. I have used it for more than 12 years. My
spouse and some of my colleagues have set up similar systems,
and they are very satisfied with them. The system enables them
to retrieve information quickly, and thus they are able to get
their work done with less delay.

Skill 13.   Set aside time each day for planning your studies.

I believe in the value of planning. I spend some time each
day thinking through what I want to accomplish the following
day or week. What does this have to do with procrastination?
The answer is that students often delay getting homework done
because they have forgotten all about it. When homework is difficult, it is conveniently forgotten — unless you include it in your
plan of *Things to Do*.

Planning helps you remember what to do, but it is also important for another reason. Most of us have many things to do

each day, usually more than we can accomplish. We live busy lives. For example, from 4:30 to 7:30 today I did the following: drove my son's playmate back to his parents' home; dropped my son off at his babysitter's home; went to the gym for a workout; went to the university to pick up my mail and do a bit of paperwork; picked up my son; went to the grocery store for a few items; and then rushed home to catch the last few innings of a World Series game. There are many other things I need and want to do. They would leave no time for writing this book. My point is that careful planning is necessary to keep track of your priorities, the time they require, and the order in which you will do them.

I recommend three techniques to students for their daily planning. First, use 3x5 index cards or something similar to list your daily schedule. I have used these cards for many years because they are easy to carry around in my shirt pocket. In the evening I make a list of everything I plan to do the following day. I list activities that will occur at a specified time — classes, meetings, phone calls — at the top of the 3x5 card. The bottom part of the card is used to list other activities: errands, people to visit, study tasks, and so forth. As I think of new things that need doing, I add them to the list. When something on the list gets done, I cross it off. At the end of the day I have a quick visual check of how much I have accomplished. Uncompleted tasks may be transferred to my 3x5 card for the next day or to another card I keep on my desk for listing tasks that can wait. Items will sometimes stay on that list for months until I get around to doing them. I cross out some of them eventually because they no longer seem necessary.

I occasionally read about a prominent person who uses notecards or something similar to list tasks to be done. Perhaps these people became prominent because they get a lot done, and perhaps they get a lot done because they plan and organize their time productively.

The second technique for planning your time is to carry around an appointment book. I recommend a little daily appointment book (mine is 4¼″ by 2¾″, called the "Aristocrat Diary" and published by the Wilson Jones Company) that you can put in your shirt pocket or purse. They can be purchased at most stationery stores. Mine has approximately an inch of blank space for each day of the year, a calendar, and space for addresses and phone numbers. I carry it around all the time so that if someone asks me when we can meet, I can check my schedule and write in the appointment on the spot.

I have known quite a few students who have missed classes, exams, or appointments because they forgot them. Sometimes they remembered what needed to be done, but they forgot the correct time and place. Of course, the reason they forgot is that they tried to rely on their memory; or they wrote the appointment on a scrap of paper which got lost.

I recall one of my graduate advisees who habitually missed appointments because he forgot about them. (He was disorganized in his studies, too.) After he had missed several appointments with me, I gave him an ultimatum. I told him that I would not schedule another meeting with him until he purchased an appointment book and showed it to me. When he had done so, I checked that he entered each of our appointments in the book. This did not solve the problem entirely, but it helped.

The third technique for planning is to organize your schedule into blocks of time. Consider first your daily schedule. For example, when I was in college, I thought of morning as a time for classes; afternoon as a time for exercise, errands, and visiting friends; and evening as a time for study and relaxation. A daily routine puts order into your life and makes it easier to plan each day's activities.

Weekly planning is also necessary. It helps you sort out your priorities so that the important things get done, and so that conflicts are avoided. For example, you might decide that you need to hold down a part-time job to support your college education. You will need to get your job schedule arranged as soon as possible, and then coordinate it with the university's schedule of courses. These course schedules are usually flexible so that you can select courses and times that fit into your job schedule. This is only possible if you do weekly planning in advance.

Finally, it is important to set aside time periodically for long-range planning. You should think through your long-term goals and possible methods for accomplishing them. Also, review your progress toward these goals. Some experts on time management recommend that you reserve time once a week for long-range planning.

References

Alan Lakein. *How To Get Control of Your Time and Your Life.* New York: Signet (New American Library), 1973.

William J. Bond. *1001 Ways To Beat the Time Trap.* New York: Frederick Fell Publishers, 1982.

These two books contain a wealth of ideas about how to manage your time effectively. Lakein's little book is a classic and covers all aspects of your life. Bond's book is also useful, but is more oriented toward adult professionals. His book will show you that time management skills you learn as a student will transfer to your eventual career.

Harold H. Bloomfield and others. *Transcendental Meditation: Discovering Inner Energy and Overcoming Stress.* New York: Dell Books, 1975.

Lawrence LeShan. *How To Meditate.* New York: Bantam Books, 1975.

These two little books contain many valuable ideas about how to organize and calm your mind in preparation for studying.

3

Active Listening And Participation In Class

If you look into a classroom, most probably you will see the teacher talking to a class of students. This is what we call _lecture_. Another possibility is that the students are talking to each other or to the teacher. They are engaged in _discussion_. A college course in which discussion dominates is usually called a seminar. The third possibility is that students are involved in _laboratory_ work, as in a chemistry lab.

Lecture, discussion, and laboratory work are the most common methods of instruction in junior high and high school, college, and graduate school. Other methods are occasionally used, for example, instruction by computer, role playing, and showing of films and filmstrips. I will concentrate in this chapter, however, on what to do during lectures and discussions because they are less structured than other methods and thus place the most demands on you as to how to respond. The first part of the chapter presents techniques for actively listening to a teacher's lecture. The second part describes techniques for increasing your active participation in a class discussion.

Getting the Most from Lectures

Skill 14. Take notes when it is important to remember what the teacher is saying.

As a professor, I know that I am required to meet my class at regularly scheduled times. However, there are very few requirements about what I should do in class. Professors largely do as they wish. The same is true of junior high and high school teachers. This situation creates a problem for you, the student. Your approach to attending class needs to be centered around the teacher's intentions: what is he or she trying to accomplish in class? Once you have analyzed the teacher's intentions, you can figure out a note-taking strategy that makes sense.

The following list of items are what teachers usually do in class:

1. Present information not in the assigned readings.
2. Explain difficult ideas in the assigned readings.
3. Explain and provide practice in new skills.
4. Conduct demonstrations (for example, a physics experiment).
5. Discuss course assignments.

When you attend class, listen carefully and judge which one of these things the teacher is doing at each point in time. This judgment will help you figure out whether you should take notes, and how extensive they should be.

Consider the first item on the list. Some teachers like to supplement the course text by presenting additional information in class. Teachers tend to be fairly critical, and so they look for gaps in the assigned text. As for myself, I have never found a text that was completely satisfactory in its coverage. I therefore spend some class time presenting ideas not in the course text.

You need to determine whether the teacher expects you to remember this additional material. Are you expected to recall it on a course exam? Are you expected to write about it in a paper? If your answer to either question is yes, obviously you should take careful notes on what the teacher says. On the other hand, you may discover that the additional material is just meant as "color" commentary on the text. The teacher does not expect you to remember it on a test.

It may be difficult for you to come straight out and ask the teacher what he or she expects you to do with this additional information. If pressed, some teachers will say that you are responsible for everything presented in the course. Your best bet might be to ask students who previously took the course whether they were held responsible for what the teacher said in class.

Suppose the teacher is trying to explain difficult ideas presented in the course text (item #2 above). As a professor, I have come to learn the "sticky" points for students in the courses I teach. For example, the concept of "statistical significance tests" in the field of social science research is very difficult for students to understand. Yet the concept is central to the field. Therefore I spend much class time explaining the meaning of statistical significance tests whenever I teach a course on research methodology.

If your teacher is trying to explain a difficult concept to the class, it is worth the effort to listen carefully. I recommend that you take notes on these explanations. If you forget what the teacher has said before you can write it down, you are probably trying to take too many notes. Listen carefully and just write down key words and phrases.

Many teachers use class time by having students practice skills taught in the course (item #3 above). Lab courses, for example, focus almost entirely on this type of activity. Math teachers often have students solve new types of math problems during class. In English classes, the teacher may engage students in practicing how to interpret poems, short stories, and other literary forms. When class time is used in this way, note taking hardly seems necessary. What is important is to actively participate in the activity that the teacher has organized. Practice the skills that you are expected to learn.

The fourth type of class activity mentioned above is for the teacher to conduct demonstrations that illustrate key ideas in the text. For example, the teacher may conduct an experiment described in your textbook. Or the teacher may show a film related to a course topic. As always, you need to analyze the teacher's intent in providing the demonstration. This will help to determine what your response should be. If the teacher expects you to be able to repeat the demonstration on your own, you should take notes on details not covered in the text. If the demonstration is only meant to illustrate the text, then careful attention without note taking should be sufficient.

Finally, let us consider item #5 above — the teacher's use of class time to present course assignments and procedures. This is when you should be listening most attentively and taking careful notes. I find, though, that many students do not take notes. They try to rely on memory alone. Consequently, they hand in assignments late, read the wrong pages in the course text, write papers that are too long or short, and so forth. I think that students are more likely to do poorly in a course if they fail to take notes on course assignments than if they neglect to take notes on a particular topic covered in class.

The teacher's instructions often occur during the last few minutes of class when many students are getting ready to leave. They are busy picking up their books so they can make a quick exit. But this is when you should be most alert. Pay careful attention to those last-minute instructions that the teacher gives just before the bell rings.

Skill 15.   *Read the assignment before coming to class.*

Teachers' lectures relate to the course text at least some of the time. Teachers know that students will criticize them if they do not make a connection between what they talk about in class and what students are required to read outside of class.

You can turn this fact to your advantage by making sure that you read the relevant assignment *before* the teacher discusses it in class. I can recall many times in college when I did not follow this simple principle. I attended the professor's lectures without having done the required reading. The professor assumed that we were already familiar from our readings with certain technical terms and ideas. Because I had not read the relevant material beforehand, I found it difficult to understand what the professor was talking about.

You will have to study the course readings sooner or later. You might as well do this study in advance of the teacher's lectures so that you can receive their full benefit. With proper preparation, lectures can help you rehearse and expand your understanding of the course content.

Skill 16.   Take selective notes on the teacher's lecture.

Note taking is a difficult process, and most students do not do it very well. For example, there is the compulsive student who takes notes on everything the teacher says. This student aims for a word-by-word transcript of the teacher's lecture. Not only is this an impossible goal, but you cannot listen very well if you are occupied with taking notes. The advantage of lectures is that they provide you the opportunity to learn by *listening* to an oral presentation. Therefore, anything that interferes with your listening (such as copious note taking) will also be detrimental to your learning. Your purpose in lectures is to listen and think. Note taking should help that process, not interfere with it.

Tape-recording the teacher's lecture, in my opinion, is an even worse strategy than copious note taking. Some students tape the teacher's lectures so that they can take it easy in class: "Let the tape recorder do the work; I'll just sit back and relax." In fact, tape recording is very time consuming if you decide to listen to the tapes later on for review purposes. Also, you are faced with the decision about how and whether to take notes while reviewing the tapes. Some teachers, by the way, do not permit students to tape-record their lectures.

An alternative to copious note taking or tape recording is to take no notes at all. This leaves you free to concentrate entirely on listening. This strategy, however, has the disadvantage that later you must rely entirely on your memory to review what the teacher said. Most of us do not have sufficient memory power for this purpose.

Your note-taking strategy should lie somewhere between the two extremes described above. I recommend *selective note taking* in which you jot down just the key terms and phrases in the teacher's lecture. These brief, selective notes should not interfere with your ability to listen to what is being said. In fact, selective note taking should intensify your listening because you will be actively searching for terms and phrases that capture the essence of the teacher's lecture.

When you review your notes at a later time, you can try to reconstruct the lecture from these brief phrases. This process requires you to *actively* review your notes. And active review of selective notes is more beneficial than passive reading of a complete lecture transcript.

Skill 17. Make a brief summary at the end of the lecture.

Sometimes a teacher will overwhelm you with information and ideas in a lecture. You may have been so busy listening and taking notes that you cannot form a "big picture" of what the lecture was about. For this reason I recommend that you take one or two minutes before you leave the classroom to write a brief summary of the lecture.

The summary need only be one or two sentences. In writing the summary, ask yourself these questions: What topics did the teacher cover today? What were the main points that he or she made? Answering the questions will help you to review the essence of the lecture quickly.

Keep the brief summary of each lecture with your lecture notes. These summaries will be very helpful when it is time to write a paper or review for tests. They provide a convenient record of what the teacher stressed in class. They should help you recall how different topics covered in the course connected to one another.

Your lecture summaries will help you remember the most significant points covered in class. They will give you clues about what to stress in studying for tests, and what ideas to include in your papers.

Skill 18.   Write your lecture notes on binder paper.

There is no point in taking lecture notes if you cannot find them later. What you need is a system for easy storage and retrieval of your notes. The system that I recommend is quite simple: keep all of your notes on standard size (8½″ x 11″) three-hole-punched paper — sometimes called "binder paper." If you use smaller-sized paper, you will need more of it, and it will be bulkier to store. Also, teacher handouts are usually on 8½″ x 11″ paper. If your notes are also on 8½″ x 11″ paper, teacher handouts are easily integrated and stored with them. If the teacher's handouts are not punched for a three-ring binder, you can buy an inexpensive paper punch and do the job yourself. Irregular-size handouts and other printed matter can be cut to 8½″ x 11″ size or taped on to blank binder paper.

You should keep everything relating to a particular course in one place. Therefore I recommend that you buy a package of individual sheets of binder paper rather than spiral-bound notebooks. The individual sheets can be put into a three-ring binder and easily integrated with handouts, journal reprints, etc. You might keep a supply of sheets of paper at the back of the binder on which to take notes. When you have filled a sheet with notes, move it to the section of the binder containing your other notes for the course.

By following this procedure, you can keep almost everything you need for all your courses in one three-ring binder. Keep each course separate from the other courses by using a binder divider, which is a sheet of stiff paper with a tab. Binder dividers can be purchased at a stationery store, or you can make them yourself. If you have a lot of material pertaining to a course, you can sort it into categories (e.g., notes, handouts, assignments) and then separate material in each category by binder dividers. Bulky or seldom-used material can be kept in file folders.

As you complete each of your courses, you will need to decide whether to save your notes, completed assignments, and other materials for future reference. I suggest you resist saving too much. Saving your course text and term papers should be sufficient. Term papers can be placed in file folders and stored in a file cabinet (see Skill 12).

Skill 19. Ask questions in class.

An unfortunate aspect of American education is that most students are afraid to ask questions in class. They are intimidated by their teachers. I must admit that a few teachers — but only a few — come across as fearsome and unapproachable. Most teachers, however, work in schools and colleges because they enjoy teaching. Much of their gratification comes from communicating knowledge in a way that students can understand. Also, consider this: if you do not understand what the teacher is talking about, you probably will tell other students that the teacher is a poor teacher, or give the course a low rating. If enough students feel the same way you do, the teacher eventually will get a bad reputation. Thus it is in the teacher's best interests to help students achieve a good understanding of the course content.

Teachers know that a good way to check students' understanding is to stop at certain points in a lecture and ask, "Any questions?" At such times you should feel free to ask a question. Even if the teacher does not formally request questions, just raise your hand if you want him or her to clarify a certain point.

With only a few exceptions, I have never been reluctant to ask questions. In fact, I have become increasingly bold about asking questions because it is such an excellent way to learn. I cannot wait until question-and-answer time when I attend workshops or listen to my colleagues' presentations. I want to ask questions to challenge the presenter's argument, to get further information, or to clarify certain points made by the presenter.

Even though I am forward about asking questions, I know that many students are afraid to do so. They do have questions to ask. That is not the problem. The problem is that they are afraid the teacher and classmates will think that their questions are stupid.

In fact, the only stupid thing about asking questions is the people who criticize students for asking questions. Occasionally when I ask a question — or a string of questions — someone will give me a puzzled or nasty look, as if to say, "Why don't you just shut up and listen to the presenter?" Rather than feel guilty, I tend to get a bit angry at the person who is trying to stifle my questions. I have every right to ask questions if I do so tactfully.

Another reason why some students are afraid to ask questions in class is that they believe the teacher will react negatively. They can imagine such put-downs as, "If you had read your assignment, you wouldn't have to ask that question," or "I thought I just explained that point," or "I don't want to answer any questions right now." The teacher who would make such a hostile or insensitive remark has a problem — not you.

I remember taking a psychology course from a professor whose trademark was that he would never answer students' questions in class. He spent most of the class time writing notes on the blackboard with his back to the students. From observing this professor's behavior in other contexts, some of us discovered that he was a rather shy person and afraid of students. We did not have a problem because we wanted to ask questions; *he* had a problem because he did not want to answer them.

Finally, some students are afraid to ask questions because they are afraid to say anything in class. If this is your problem, please read the class discussion skills presented later in the chapter.

I emphasize question-asking here and elsewhere (see Skills 25, 27, and 64) because it is so critical to effective study. If a question comes to your mind, it means that you are *actively* thinking about the course content. And the more you actively process the content, the more you will learn. Remember — smart students ask lots of questions.

Participating in Class Discussions

Sooner or later you will take a course that emphasizes discussion. If a course relies almost exclusively on discussion, it is called a *seminar*. Even in large college courses with hundreds of students enrolled, there usually is a *discussion section* once a week to supplement the professor's lectures. I have seen large lecture courses, both at Berkeley and at Harvard, with four or five hundred students. The discussion sections for these courses are usually limited to 20 or 25 students, and there may be 20 or so such sections at different times of the day and week. Typically you can select any discussion section if there is still an opening in it at the time you enroll.

The discussion sections are usually led by doctoral students, who are paid to perform this task. When I was a doctoral student at Berkeley, I worked part time one year as a discussion section leader for a large undergraduate course called *Psychology of Human Adjustment.*

When it comes to participating in a formal class discussion, we all react differently. Some students shine in discussions. They just like to talk, or they view discussion as a forum for expressing their ideas. Other students are just the opposite; they dread speaking in public. They remain silent at all costs, or if compelled to speak, their throats go dry, they speak haltingly, and their voices crack and falter.

I am not certain that the ability to participate in class discussions is related to academic brilliance. I knew some very bright students at Harvard who wrote great papers and who performed well on exams. Yet these same students were so shy that they never spoke in class. Conversely, I also knew average students who were very confident and poised in any speaking situation.

You need to analyze where you fit among these types of students. If you participate with ease in a formal discussion, all is well. If you do not, you need to take stock of yourself. Is your reluctance or inability to speak in groups a problem for you? The symptoms are certainly obvious: a sensation of anxiety at the mere thought of speaking before a group; a feeling that you always say the wrong thing in discussions; or the realization that you always think of something to say *after* the discussion has ended. If any of these symptoms characterize you, please read on.

Skill 20. Read the assignment beforehand so you can contribute to class discussions.

If you are hesitant about participating in discussions, you will find it helpful to read the assignment thoroughly beforehand. You will be able to follow the drift of the discussion, and if the teacher calls upon you to participate, you are likely to have a pertinent fact or opinion at your disposal. In fact, one of the best cures for a case of speaking jitters is careful preparation beforehand. This point is elaborated further in the discussion of the next skill.

Skill 21. Rehearse what you want to say before you say it.

I feel comfortable in discussion situations and, in fact, I regularly teach a course for teachers on how to use the discussion method. Feeling comfortable in discussions does not mean I blurt out whatever comes to mind. Instead, I first listen carefully to everything that is being said. Eventually an idea will enter my mind. Next, I will say the idea to myself to "hear" how it sounds. I may do this several times to see whether it continues to make sense. If it does not sound right, I will keep my idea to myself. However, if the idea continues to make sense as I rehearse it, I will wait for a suitable opportunity to speak up.

Finding "air time" in a discussion requires practice. With other students and the teacher talking, it is difficult to find an appropriate entry point for your own remarks. I try to wait for lulls in the discussion, and signal that I have something to say — by sitting alert and by engaging the discussion leader and other participants in eye contact. I find, too, that my words carry more weight if I hold back until more forceful participants have "let off steam."

The next time you participate in a discussion, I suggest you try these steps: listen attentively, get an idea, rehearse it mentally, and signal non-verbally to others that you have something to say. These steps may be sufficient to get you verbally involved in the discussion.

Skill 22. If you do not feel comfortable expressing an opinion, ask a question.

I would caution you against trying to "score points" in a discussion. If you try too hard to appear knowledgeable, the teacher and other students will see through your ploy. It is best to express an idea or opinion in a serious, natural way. If you feel unsure of yourself but still wish to contribute to the discussion, why not ask a good question? People appreciate someone who asks thoughtful questions.

As an example of what I mean, the other day several of my colleagues and I discussed a proposed research project. The colleagues were professors from several colleges and universities around the state, and they spent quite a bit of time trying to impress each other. One of my co-workers, I noticed, carefully listened to the others. At appropriate pauses in the conversation, he asked several of his colleagues to expand on things they had said. This professor made a better impression by careful listening and questioning than if he had tried to toot his own horn.

So, the next time you are in a class discussion, try asking a pertinent question. Direct it to the teacher or to another student. I know from experience that teachers look favorably on students who ask good questions. Like most people, they feel less favorable towards students who monopolize discussion time with their own views.

Skill 23. Improve your speaking skills by taking a communications course.

If you get uptight about speaking in your classes, you should consider doing something about it. The problem may follow you into later life. For example, I heard recently about a young doctor who is doing a residency in pediatrics. He is having a terrible time because he occasionally has to give talks about new developments in his medical specialty. He knows the research literature thoroughly, but is petrified at the thought of standing up and speaking before an audience.

This is not an isolated example. Sales people, investment brokers, business managers of all types, teachers, and many other professional workers need to speak to groups. In fact, career advancement may hinge on this ability. Thus, if speaking to others emerges as a problem for you in school, you should think seriously about overcoming it.

Many high schools and colleges offer courses to help students who feel uncomfortable speaking in group situations. The courses are different from the usual public speaking courses. They are designed specifically for students who are very anxious about speaking in public. In college, such courses are usually offered by professors in the speech or counseling departments. You will be in a congenial environment with other students and faculty who understand your problem.

The approach used in these courses is to *gradually* develop your skill and confidence in speaking in various situations. This is done by having you engage in brief, non-threatening exercises. As your confidence builds, more sophisticated skills are developed. This approach is similar to that used in Dale Carnegie courses around the country for professional people whose job responsibilities require them to speak in public.

4

Reading Textbooks Effectively

To read textbooks effectively, you must be *thinking about* what you are reading. The skills required to read this way are rarely taught in school.

Students are taught to read in elementary school. However, they do not have enough vocabulary or cognitive ability at that point to analyze much of what they read.

Many high school teachers believe that their only responsibility is to teach subject matter — English, biology, history, mathematics, and so forth. They assume that students have the necessary skills to read textbooks in these subjects. The assumption is unjustified. Reading skills taught in elementary school are not adequate for the complex task of studying textbooks in junior high school, high school and college.

Beginning in junior high or high school, you will spend much of your homework time reading books and journal articles. Your teachers will give you regular reading assignments in textbooks. If your study skills are deficient, you will read the assignments too slowly and remember too little.

Study skills in reading are especially important because many textbooks are not well written. I do not know anyone who reads textbooks for pleasure. They are usually dull and pedantic. They cover a large number of topics at a superficial level. Many of them are written by professors to impress other professors. They are not written to make it easy for students to learn.

If a textbook is poorly written, what do you do? You have a right to feel frustrated, but do not feel defeated. The constructive thing to do is to develop an effective strategy to deal with difficult reading material. The study skills presented in this chapter are designed to help you replace frustration with a feeling of positive control over the reading process.

The study skills are described in the context of reading textbooks. However, the skills apply equally well to reading magazine articles, encyclopedias, pamphlets, and other material.

A Strategy for Reading Textbooks

The worst way to read textbooks is to read each page without actively reflecting on what is being read. A tell-tale sign that a student is doing this is to see him or her flipping pages to check how many more pages are left to be read. Students who have not developed good reading skills often do this.

A slightly better way to read textbooks is to underline words and phrases as one reads along. Some students develop elaborate means of underlining with different color pens to underline different types of content. Underlining is somewhat helpful because it requires the student to identify the important information in the text.

Writing notes in the margin of the textbook accomplishes the same basic purpose as underlining. These notes usually repeat key concepts and facts that appear in the text.

Underlining and note taking are all right, but they do not get you to think in a way that leads to superior grades. The following study strategy is much more effective and can be used to read virtually any textbook, chapter by chapter. The strategy consists of these four steps:

Step 1. Scan each chapter to see how it is organized into sections.

Step 2. Study one section at a time. Thoroughly process each section before going on to the next section.

Step 3. After each section, think of several questions about the content presented in it. Write each question and briefly answer it in your head.

Step 4. When you finish the chapter, make a few notes on what it was about. Also, briefly review your questions and asterisk those that seem most important.

This strategy is not difficult to use. The only step that requires real skill is Step 3. It takes time to learn how to generate good questions.

I used this strategy extensively when I was a student at Harvard and at Berkeley. There is also research evidence that supports its effectiveness.

Now let's consider the four steps in more detail, in Skills 24 through 33.

Skill 24. Start your study of a textbook chapter by reading the headings and subheadings.

Most students are "straight line" readers. In other words, their reading pattern follows a straight line from beginning to end. They start a textbook assignment by reading the first sentence, and then read each following sentence, one by one, until they complete the assignment.

Smart students read textbooks differently. They start by reading all of the headings in the chapter. Most textbooks use three types of headings. The most general are the *main headings*, which are usually centered between the right and left margins and printed in large, bold type. *Subheadings* usually appear at the left side of the page and are printed in smaller, less bold type. Subheadings describe topics that are subsumed under a more general topic stated in the main heading. The third type of heading is the *paragraph heading*. These headings, which appear at the start of a paragraph, are used if the textbook author wishes to identify several distinct topics covered under a subheading. I generally do not include paragraph headings in my initial study of a chapter. Instead, I examine paragraph headings when I actually start reading each section of the chapter.

The task of reading chapter headings takes only a few minutes, yet it gives the student a good overview of what the chapter is about. The next step is to develop an understanding of the logical basis for the headings. Why did the author make some topics into main headings and others into subheadings? To answer this question, I suggest you jot down the headings and subheadings on a sheet of paper. This enables you to see them all together rather than interspersed throughout the chapter. For example, here are the main headings and subheadings for this chapter:

Introduction

A Strategy for Reading Textbooks
>   Read headings — Generate questions — Write definitions — Graphs, tables, diagrams — Write down questions —Asterisk important questions — Time lines and concept trees — Investigate other sources — Normal reading rate — Make own notes

Scholarly and Research Texts
>   Make notes on assertions

Literature
>   Attend to literary aspects — Read critical reviews

Science and Math Textbooks
>   Don't skip anything — Get tutorial help — Make sketches of problems

It took just a few minutes to go through the chapter and jot down the headings. Note that I saved time by shortening the wording of the subheadings.

Assuming I was reading this chapter for a course, here is how I would think about it using my notes on the headings:

"Hmm. This chapter concentrates on techniques for studying textbooks. I know I'll have to read a lot of textbooks in college, so I'll see if I can pick up some useful tips. The chapter starts with a general introduction — I wonder what that's about — maybe it's about how studying textbooks fits into the big picture of going to college. Hmm, the biggest section seems to be on some sort of general strategy for textbook study. I'll probably spend most of my time reading this section ... I wonder what time lines and concept trees are. The last three sections are on how to read specific kinds of textbooks. Since I'm an English major, I should pay special attention to the section on literature."

This process of thinking about what the headings mean sheds light on the entire chapter. Yet it takes only a few minutes of your time. Note, too, that analysis of chapter headings breaks you of the habit of linear reading. To use this skill, you need to skip around the chapter, actively looking for headings that key you to the important information rather than reading sentences one by one.

Skill 25.   *After reading each section of a chapter, generate questions about its content.*

The content that follows each main heading of a chapter can be considered a separate "section." If the sections are long (more than four or five pages), you may wish to consider the content under each subheading as a separate section.

After reading each section, write down several questions about its content. This is the most important recommendation in this chapter. It is important for two reasons. First, generating questions is the best way I know to *actively* study a textbook. Second, generating questions initiates the process of preparing for exams, course papers, and other assignments.

What types of questions should you generate? As you read each section of a chapter, ask yourself, "What facts and ideas do I need to remember from what I just read?" Then generate specific questions about these facts and ideas. You can test yourself later by answering these self-generated questions. As an example, consider the preceding section of this book — Skill 24. Here are some questions I would generate after reading it:

1. What is "straight line reading" and what do smart students do differently?
2. What are the three types of chapter headings?
3. Why is it worthwhile to jot down main headings and subheadings?

You should generate questions whose answer includes several important facts and ideas. A fact or idea may be important because:

1. The teacher has discussed it in class, or has stated that he or she considers it important.
2. You personally think it is pertinent to the larger topic being studied.
3. You have reason to think you might be tested on it or need to refer to it in writing a paper.
4. It appeals to you. Perhaps it supports your beliefs or it gives you a new insight.

You can use any or all of these criteria to decide which facts and ideas in a reading assignment are worth turning into questions. Your ability to make these decisions will improve with practice. You will become more skillful at sensing which facts and ideas will need to be recalled at a later time.

I suggest you write questions instead of taking extensive notes. The questions can be written on binder pages (see Skill 18) so they can fit inside a three-ring binder with your lecture notes and class handouts. A good idea is to draw a line down the middle of the page. Write questions on the left side and brief answers on the right side.

Skill 26. Write definitions of key terms.

Learning new terminology is a major aspect of study. You will usually encounter some new terms in each reading assignment. In fact, all academic disciplines — for example, chemistry, history, literature, geography — are alike in their use of specialized terminology. What is the best way to learn this terminology?

A well-written textbook will simplify your study efforts by highlighting each new term in boldface type, by defining it in the text, or by providing a glossary (usually at the end of the book) in which each term is defined. If your textbook does not have these features, you will need to create them yourself. As you read each section, make note of the new terms. You can either write down each term, or incorporate it in a question, as these examples illustrate:

What does "laissez-faire economics" mean?

What is the Federal Reserve Board?

The textbook author will sometimes offer a formal definition of the term. But there will be instances where you will need to construct your own definition using the information provided in the text.

Learning a definition exactly as stated in the textbook is not effective. This type of rote learning is quickly forgotten. It is more effective to paraphrase the definition so that it makes sense to you personally.

As a professor, I know that learning new terminology is a substantial part of most college courses. Yet many students skip over new terms in their reading assignments without making special note of them. They may read a term and the accompanying definition, but they do not mentally process this new information. If you want to become a better student, here is what you need to do:

1. Identify each new term in your reading assignment.

2. Determine how the term relates to the larger topic you are studying.

3. Think about the phenomena to which the term refers.

For terms which refer to a concept, it is helpful to think of examples and non-examples of the concept. For example, in learning the term "metaphor," you should make up examples of metaphors. Also, make up non-examples which are similar to metaphors but which lack one or more of their critical characteristics.

Your definitions of terms in a chapter can be written on binder pages (see Skill 18) and included with the questions you have generated for the chapter.

Skill 27. *Ask yourself questions about relationships depicted in graphs, tables, and diagrams.*

You will often run into numerical data when reading textbooks. The data are usually discussed in the text. For example, an account of the weather in Canada may describe how different regions of the country differ in climate.

Often the numerical data are presented in a graph or table as well. For example, the textbook may present a chart showing the average annual temperature and amount of rainfall in each Canadian province.

If you are not mathematically minded, you may tend to skip over these pictorial aids. However, you do so at your own risk. The ability to interpret graphs and tables is required in many courses.

In studying graphs and tables, I find it helpful to ask myself two questions:

1. What are the "things" (sometimes called "variables") that are shown in the graph or table? Graphs and tables usually show data about two "things."

2. Once I figure out the things being depicted in the graph or table, I ask myself, What is the relationship between these two things?

If I can answer these two questions, I know that I understand the graph or table. I can check my understanding further by reading the author's discussion in the text. Unless the data are critical to the topic being discussed, the teacher probably will not expect you to remember the actual numbers (years, amounts, quantities, ratios, etc.). It is usually just necessary to be able to *describe* the relationship between the "things" depicted in the table or graph.

Figure 1 is a life expectancy graph that appeared in a high school science textbook.

Note that the graph has "bars" that differ in height. Each bar shows an amount of something.

Figure I. Bar Graph Showing Changes in Life Expectancy

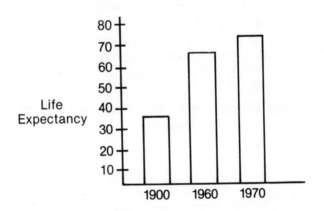

Here are the questions that I would ask myself about this graph, and also my answers:

1.   What things are shown in this graph? (Life expectancy, which is the number of years that an average person lives; and selected years from 1900 to 1970.)

2.   What is the relationship between these two things? (Life expectancy has increased greatly from 1900 to 1970. In 1900 the average person lived to be about 35 years old, and in 1970 the average person lived to be over 70 years old.

Sometimes a graph just uses a straight line to show the relationship between two things. Figure 2 is a line graph depicting the use of national parks over a period of years. It is taken from an American history book.

Figure 2. Line Graph of Use of National Parks in Selected Years

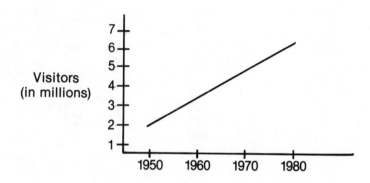

Here are my questions and answers about this graph:

1. What things are shown in this graph? (Number of people; and selected years from 1950 to 1980.)

2. What is the relationship between these two things? (The number of people who used national parks increased enormously from 1950 to 1980.)

A table presents information in different columns. A table usually contains more detailed numerical data than a graph, as shown in the example in Table 2 from a health textbook.

Table 2. Typical Table Showing Average Weight
(in Pounds) by Age

Age	Boys	Girls
11 years	87	83
12	92	88
13	100	95
14	103	100
15	120	110
16	138	115
17	145	125
18	150	127

My questions about this table are:

1. What things are shown in this table? (The average weights of boys at different ages; and the average weights of girls at different ages.)

2. What is the relationship between these two things? (Boys weigh a bit more than girls at age 11, but by age 18 they weigh a lot more. Also, the difference starts increasing a lot about age 15.

3. What is the relationship between weight and age in this table? (Both boys and girls gain weight each year.)

Diagrams are similar to graphs and tables in that they show "things" and the relationship between them. However, diagrams are different in that they do not present numerical data. Figure 3 is a diagram from a textbook on world culture.

Figure 3. Diagram of a Technology Chain

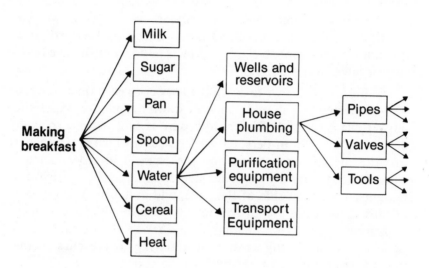

You can study a diagram by asking the same questions you would ask about tables and graphs: What are the "things" represented in the diagram? What is the relationship between them? For example, I would make up these questions and answers for the above diagram:

1. What things are shown in this diagram? (A simple example of daily living; and all the technology required for it.)

2. What is the relationship between the parts of the diagram? (Each piece of technology requires other technology to produce it; so we could not have water in our houses unless there was a long chain of technology to provide all the necessary equipment.)

Skill 28. Write down the questions you have generated.

I recommend that you make a written record of the questions that come to your mind as you read each section of a textbook assignment. You can use the written record later to quiz yourself in preparation for course exams. Your written questions also serve as a collection of notes about the textbook. If you have done the job right, key facts and ideas will have been incorporated in the questions.

Should you also write down the answer to each question you have generated? Or should you write down the page on which the answer can be found? Either procedure is satisfactory, so your decision is a matter of personal preference. My own preference is to write the section heading and the pages it includes. Then I write the questions I have generated for that section. I leave a margin on the right side of the page, and in it I jot a few words or phrases that are the answer to the question. When I wish to quiz myself, I cover up the margin and try to answer each question. I then check my answer by referring to the cues in the margin. If in doubt, I refer back to the textbook.

Figure 4 is a reproduction of two pages from a typical biology textbook. In Table 3, preceding the figure, I have presented the questions I wrote concerning these textbook pages.

Note that I generated five questions for each page of the textbook. This number of questions may seem high. It is appropriate, however, given the amount of technical material that is presented in the textbook.

Writing questions like those in Table 3 takes no more time than taking notes on the text. Writing questions is even better than taking notes, though. They help cue your thinking to the questions that your teacher may use to test you on the material in the textbook.

Sometimes textbooks themselves have questions to aid your study and review. Pay particular attention to them. Question 11 in Table 3, for example, is taken directly from the illustration in the biology textbook.

Table 3.
Questions Generated about a Section of a Biology Textbook

page 93   Answers

1. What are cells?   Building blocks of living
                                                    things.

2. What is the Cell   (See preceding chapter.)
   Theory?

3. What does *dissect*   Cut up into smaller parts —
   mean?   done so you can see cells
                                                   under microscope and do
                                                   chemical tests on them.

4. What are 3 facts   Most look the same; have
   about cells?   chemical action in them;
                                                   chemical actions explain life
                                                   functions.

5. What does a cell   See figure 94-1. Most cells
   look like?   look alike.

page 94

6. How do plant and   Only plant cells have a wall.
   animal cells differ?

7. What is chlorophyll?   A green cell chemical
                                                   contained in chloroplasts.

8. What are 3 things   Cytoplasm (a thick fluid);
   inside cell mem-   nucleus (darker object);
   branes?   vacuoles (filled with water and
                                                   dissolved chemicals).

9. What is protoplasm?   Another word for "living
                                                   matter."

10. Why did Hooke just   The living matter had died.
    see the walls of cork
    cells?

11. Is it correct to show   Yes. The plant cell shown in
    the plant cell without   Figure 94-1 is no longer a
    chloroplasts in   living cell.
    Figure 94-1? Why?

Figure 4. Reproduction of two pages from a typical
Biology Textbook

15

TARGET
What can we see inside the cell?

A Look Inside the Cells

1. PUTTING THE EVIDENCE TOGETHER

Look at a brick wall from afar. It looks solid. Now come closer and look again. What do you see? You will probably notice that it is made of many bricks, each identical to one another. In the same way, all plants and animals are made of cells, the building blocks of all living things.

Many years have passed since the Cell Theory was announced in 1838. Since that time, as you can imagine, thousands of scientists have studied cells. Better microscopes have been built. Thousands of plants and animals have been *dissected*. As we learned earlier, to dissect is to cut up into smaller parts. These smaller parts could be examined with the new and better microscopes. Also many chemical tests have been made on cells. When we put all the facts together, we can be sure of three things:

1. In general, most cells have the same appearance.
2. There are chemical actions taking place in all cells.
3. These chemical actions explain the life functions.

2. WHAT DOES A CELL LOOK LIKE?

Although there are many kinds of dogs, you can easily describe in a general way what a dog—any dog—looks like. You can then go on to tell the difference between a shepherd and a collie. But, in general, all dogs look alike. The same is true of cells. Plant cells differ somewhat from animal cells. In plants, there are many kinds of cells; in animals, also, there are many kinds of cells. But we can still describe a *typical* cell, a cell which in general is like all cells. The two diagrams in Fig. 94-1 show typical plant and animal cells.

93

Figure 4, continued

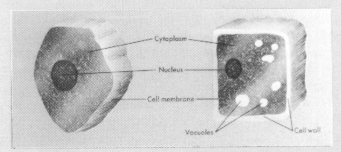

Fig. 94–1
Typical cells and their parts. Is it correct to show the plant cell without chloroplasts? Explain.

3. PLANT CELL OR ANIMAL CELL?

The cells Hooke saw seemed to have a boundary or wall. We call the outside of the cell the CELL WALL. Just inside the cell wall is another, thinner boundary called the CELL MEMBRANE. Compare the animal cell with the plant cell. Both cells have a cell membrane, but one chief difference between the two is that only the plant cell has a cell wall. In Fig. 94–1 a non-green plant cell is shown. Such cells are found in roots and stems. Other cells in leaves contain a green coloring. This green coloring comes from the chemical CHLOROPHYLL. Chlorophyll is contained in small, ball-shaped objects in the cell called CHOROPLASTS (KLOR-uh-plasts). (See Fig. 89–1, which shows plant cells of this type.)

YOU NOW KNOW

► Plant cells differ from animal cells in that they have a cell wall out-side of the cell membrane.
► Some plant cells have chloroplasts which contain chlorophyll. Such cells are green.
► Cells have length, width and thickness.

4. INSIDE THE CELL

Just inside the cell membrane is a thick fluid very much like egg-white. This is the CYTOPLASM (SY-tow-plazm). Somewhere in the cytoplasm there appears a darker, ball-shaped object called the NUCLEUS (NEW-klee-us). Also inside the cytoplasm there are one or more "spaces" called VACUOLES (VAK-u-olz). Actually, these spaces are not empty. They are filled with water and dissolved chemicals. For a long while, living matter was called PROTOPLASM (PRO-tow-plazm). Today, we simply call it *living matter*.

When Hooke first saw cork cells, he saw only the cell walls, for the living matter had died. By using fresh material, we can see the living matter of plants and animals.

Reproduced by permission from: J. M. Oxenhorn and M. N. Idelson, *The Materials of Life*. New York: Globe Book Company, Inc., 1975, pp. 93-94.

Skill 29. Asterisk your most important questions for intensive review.

A useful way to further your mental processing of a textbook is to make judgments about which facts and ideas are most important. I suggest you do this after completing each chapter. Look through all of the questions you have generated, and decide which are most important. Place an asterisk next to the questions you have selected.

To avoid asterisking every question, impose a limit on yourself. For example, you might limit yourself to asterisking no more than one fourth of the total number of questions. Suppose you generated 40 questions about the facts and ideas in a particular chapter. Using the above guideline, you would asterisk no more than 10 of these questions.

The advantage of this mental exercise is that it gets you to think more deeply about the textbook content. All knowledge is not of equal value. In this chapter, for example, some of the techniques I presented are more important than others, and it is helpful for you to realize this. In addition, the process of deciding which facts and ideas are most important to remember will probably help you recall *all* the facts and ideas covered by your questions. This is because you have to review everything in order to establish priorities.

Skill 30. Use time lines and concept trees to organize your textbook study.

Time lines and concept trees are most useful for helping you to see the "big picture." Therefore, it is unlikely that you will use them in the process of studying a single section of a textbook chapter. They are generally used to organize the important content of an entire chapter, or perhaps a series of chapters.

You can get bogged down studying factual details unless you relate them to a larger structure. For example, if you are studying a lot of historical events, you can place them on a time line.

The advantage of a time line is that it helps you form a visual image of how events relate to each other. Figure 5 is an example of a time line.

Figure 5. Time Line Summarizing Historical Events

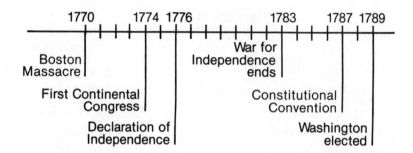

This time line helps you see the sequence of related events in the establishment of our government. A visual aid like this is easier to comprehend and recall than taking notes on a textbook chapter.

Concept trees are another useful visual aid for depicting the structure of textbook content. They are especially helpful for understanding concepts that are in a superordinate-subordinate relationship to each other.

To illustrate how concept trees work, I will refer to a high school English textbook that I looked at recently. One chapter discussed the elements of a story. If you just made a list of the elements, the list might look like this:

plot	time
problem	place
conflict	dialogue
resolution	hero and heroine
characters	minor characters
setting	events

This list is not organized in a meaningful way. Figure 6 demonstrates how this information can be organized using a concept tree.

Figure 6. Concept Tree of the Elements of a Story

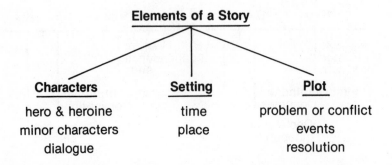

Another example of how a concept tree works can be obtained by referring back to Figure 4, which reproduces two pages from a biology textbook. The following concepts are presented in the text:

cell wall

cell membrane

cytoplasm

nucleus

vacuoles

chloroplasts

chlorophyll

Figure 7 shows how this list can be organized using a concept tree.

Figure 7. Concept Tree Showing the Parts of a Cell

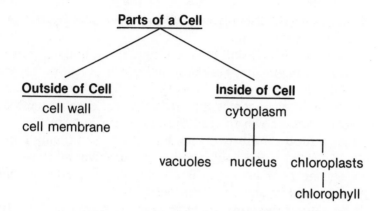

You will probably find it easier to recall a time line or concept tree than a sentence or paragraph. Unless you have a photographic memory, it is very difficult to form a picture of lines of text. Time lines and concept trees, however, form a picture in your mind's eye. What I do is first recall the outline and boxes that make up the time line or concept tree. Then I try to fill in the boxes or other "place holders" one by one. This is a lot easier than trying to recall a set of events or concepts scattered through a textbook.

In addition to improving recall, time lines and concept trees have the advantage of requiring you to actively process the textbook content. You need to search through the text to identify relevant concepts or events, and then you need to decide which are sufficiently important to place in a time line or concept tree. I cannot emphasize enough the principle that the more you interact with the text, the better you will comprehend and recall it.

Time lines and concept trees are less helpful if you include a lot of concepts or events in them. A time line or concept tree should be kept simple so that your eye can take it in at a single glance. Seven concepts or events in a single visual display is probably a good upper limit.

Skill 31. Investigate several sources on the same topic.

When I am confused by a textbook, I find it very useful to investigate different sources that cover the same content. Each source discusses the topic from a different perspective, and that is what I find so helpful.

I can illustrate this skill by referring to its natural occurrence in daily life. I might first hear of a major news event on my car radio while driving home from work. I get another perspective on the event when it comes time to watch the evening news on TV. Next I settle down to read the newspaper and, in the process, I get a third exposure to what happened. And finally I read about the event from still another perspective in a weekly newsmagazine such as *Time*. Each perspective reinforces and deepens my understanding of the event.

Why not put the same principle to work in your studies? Instead of relying on a single source (the textbook assigned by the teacher), you can look for other books and journal articles on the same topic. Popular subjects are usually covered by many textbooks. For example, there are at least 50 different textbooks currently available for the introductory college course in Psychology.

You can also supplement your reading with other experiences, for example: seeing a play or movie on the subject, going to a museum, talking to an expert, or visiting a place being studied.

It would be unrealistic to read multiple sources on every topic that you study in school. I recommend instead that you reserve this technique for difficult but essential topics. For example, calculus is a difficult course for many students. I know, too, that some calculus textbooks are much easier to study than others. If your teacher assigns a difficult calculus textbook, you should look around for an easier textbook as a supplemental source for study.

Another option to consider in studying a difficult section of your textbook is to read it two or three times. This is what most students do. But in approximately the same amount of time you can read a second source on the topic. Which procedure is more effective? I do not know of evidence relating to this question, so I cannot give you a definite answer. When confronted with really difficult content, my own preference is to: 1) read the assigned source, 2) read another source, and then 3) re-read the assigned source.

How do you locate other textbooks that cover the same topics? Your school library or local bookstore should have a copy of *Books in Print,* one volume of which is a subject index. If you look up your course subject in the index, you should find a list of several textbooks. Another technique is to look up the subject in the library's card catalog. The catalog will tell you what books on the subject are contained in the library.

If you are interested in locating journal articles on specific topics, I suggest you ask a librarian for help. Librarians know about many published indexes in the academic disciplines. The indexes list every significant journal article on a particular topic that was published within a given time period.

Skill 32. *Read at your normal rate of speed.*

Some students worry that they do not read fast enough. They hear about students who read 1,000 or 2,000 words per minute, and feel that maybe this is the competitive edge they lack.

I recommend that you not worry about your reading speed if you can read at least 300 words a minute with good comprehension. I know that I can read very fast when necessary, but most of the time I read at an average rate (approximately a page a minute). I read technical writing *very slowly,* and usually will re-read difficult sections several times. My reading rate for pleasure reading is also fairly slow; I like to appreciate what I read. And yet I earned good grades at Harvard. The important point is that you read at a rate that is comfortable for you. Avoid the trap of comparing yourself with others. You may need to spend more time doing your reading assignments than another student, but that does not matter. What counts is how much you learn, not how long it takes to learn it.

Keep in mind, too, that reading comprehension is more important than reading rate. Your comprehension of what you read will greatly affect your school performance, but reading rate will not. This is why the skills that I present in this chapter emphasize how to actively process textbook content. Active mental processing is closely related to reading comprehension.

Having minimized the importance of reading rate, I wish to note one exception. Reading rate will interfere with your studies if you read most things very slowly — at a rate of 200 words or less. Students who vocalize (sound out) everything they read have a reading rate problem. The same is true of students who read each word separately — much like beginning readers do. These students should seek professional help. Reading rate is a skill, and reading experts know how to train students in it. For example, they sometimes use machines to train your eyes to move more quickly over lines of text and to prevent you from vocalizing. This type of professional help is available at many study skill centers.

Skill 33. Rely on your own notes and questions, not on other students' work.

I will never forget my first year of graduate school at Berkeley. My classmates and I were given a huge reading list and told that we would be tested on it at the end of the school year. Reeling from the shock, we were relieved to learn that students from previous years had made extensive typed notes on most of the assigned readings. A few "fortunate" students in our class had access to these notes.

Several of us decided to make a systematic effort to collect all of the notes, so that we could make them available to everyone. Our thinking was that the notes would provide a helpful shortcut to studying our awesome reading list. A few other students and I spent a substantial amount of time collecting, duplicating, and selling at cost the notes to our classmates.

The notes were of little help, as it turned out. In many cases we had a harder time understanding the notes than the textbook or journal to which they referred. The problem was that the notes reflected other students' mental processing, not our own. It was necessary for each of us to read each book and article on the reading list, to generate our own questions, and to make our own notes.

I learned from this experience that the *active mental processing* involved in note taking is much more important than the notes themselves. The only way to engage these processes is to read and think about the textbook material on your own. Some textbooks now provide summaries (a form of notes) and questions at the end of each chapter. Even when these are available, I recommend that you generate your own questions and make your own notes; that is the best way to get your thought processes actively engaged. You can use end-of-chapter aids and other students' notes and questions as an additional check on your own thinking.

Scholarly and Research Texts

You may be expected to read primary sources in some of your courses. The term *primary sources* refers to documents in which researchers and scholars report original discoveries, theories, and interpretations. For example, an anthropologist's report on Sumatra, based on his or her fieldwork, would be a primary source. A journal report of a psychological experiment on hypnotic suggestibility is another example. A book in which the author sets out his or her own theory of how capitalism functions in a democratic society would also be considered a primary source.

Most textbooks, in contrast, are *secondary sources*. They are based on the textbook author's review and interpretation of primary source material. For example, you might read in a history textbook about the atomic bombing of Hiroshima and Nagasaki, and its significance in ending World War II. The textbook author probably collected material for his or her account by reading the writings of professional historians who collected and interpreted the available historical evidence. These writings would be considered primary source documents. The historical evidence itself (e.g., eyewitness accounts, military plans, newspaper accounts) would be the ultimate primary sources. Your "secondary source" textbook, then, is several levels removed from the actual event, as shown below:

Event of
Historical Interest

Eyewitness Accounts,
Official Documents, etc.

Newspaper Articles

Historical Research
About the Event

Textbooks for Students

Some of your teachers will want you to have the experience of reading primary source documents. This is particularly likely when you take courses in college and graduate school.

At this point you are probably asking yourself: "Should I study primary sources any differently than I would the typical textbook?" My opinion is that, yes, you do need to study primary sources using a slightly different approach. The following skill is particularly useful for organizing your study of a primary source document. It recommends a special kind of note taking when you are reading primary source material. (The other techniques covered in this chapter apply, too.)

Skill 34. Make notes on the major assertions and conclusions in primary source documents.

Most authors of primary source documents make assertions and cite findings of one sort or another. They may advance a new theory to explain observed phenomena. They may claim to have discovered a new principle or relationship based on their research. Or they may offer criticisms of previous assertions made by others. After an initial reading of a primary source document, I find it very helpful to make a summary list of the assertions and conclusions that the author has put forth. This task stimulates me to actively review the document and results in a convenient summary of what it is about.

The next step is to take notes on the evidence or arguments, if any, that the author used to support each assertion and conclusion. This task requires me to search through the primary source document looking for evidence and arguments. In the process of doing this, I get a much better idea of how the document is organized. Next, I make a few notes on whether I agree with the author's assertions, claims, evidence, and arguments.

The final step in my study of a primary source document is to make comparisons between it and other reading assignments in the course. This step is very important because teachers, more often than not, will ask you to make such comparisons in your papers and exams.

The process of making comparisons is important for another reason, too, Scholars and researchers do not work in a vacuum. Their research and writings often build upon or refute the work of their predecessors and colleagues. Therefore, most scholarship and research within an academic discipline is interrelated. Similar relationships are found across disciplines, too, because they often deal with the same phenomena. For example, language development in young children is currently an important topic of research for linguists, psychologists, sociologists, and educators. If you make explicit comparisons between a particular primary source and other documents you have read, you are more likely to see these interrelationships.

Here is a summary of the above steps:

Step 1. Read through the primary source document to get an initial idea of what it is about.

Step 2. List the author's major claims and conclusions.

Step 3. Take notes on the evidence and arguments that the author used to support his or her assertions and conclusions. Also make notes of your reactions to the validity and meaning of the author's evidence and arguments.

Step 4. Make comparisons between this primary source document and other documents and textbooks you have read.

These steps may be sufficient to guide your study of a primary source document. I recommend, though, that you also consider generating some questions about the document. (See Skills 25 and 27 for suggestions about generating questions on your reading.)

Examples of primary sources can be found in the high school textbook *Idea and Action in World Cultures.* The book contains many descriptions of cultures by anthropologists who observed them over time.

One part of the book makes the *assertion* that unique behavior patterns can be observed in any culture. These behavior patterns are used over and over again by people from that culture. They differ from the behavior observed in people who are not part of the culture.

To support the assertion about behavior patterns, the textbook presents the notes (primary source documents) of an anthropologist who observed the Bedouins over time. The Bedouins are a desert people who live in the Middle East. Figure 8 presents some of the primary source material as it appeared in the textbook.

Figure 8. Example of Primary Source Material in a Textbook

Anthropologist F. S. Vidal lived in Saudi Arabia among Bedouins, the desert people of the Middle East. In the accounts which follow, he describes patterns of action which he himself observed during the time he spent with the Bedouins.

In the Bedouin camp, one of the children saw a stranger approaching on a camel. The men and the children stood in front of the tent to watch him arrive. The women and older girls hurried away into the women's section. All could see that the stranger was a Bedouin by his clothing. He wore a red checkered head cloth held by a rope around it, a long white shirt, and a dark brown cloak. Also, they knew he must be an eastern Arab by the way his long hair was braided and because he rode sitting high on the center of the camel's hump and not way back over the hump as the southerners did. But they couldn't yet see the camel's brand marks, so they couldn't tell the man's tribe. He approached slowly from the open side of the tent, which among the Mutair always faces south. Also, he did not approach in a straight line but in a zig-zag fashion, coming closer all the time.

When the stranger got closer, it was seen by his camel's brand that he also was of the Mutair, but from another clan. No one in the camp knew the man personally. But he was hailed and asked into the tent.
"The peace be upon you."
"And upon you the peace."
"God willing you did not get tired."
"It was not in vain." (This is a way of saying, "I may be very tired, but it was worth getting tired in order to now enjoy your company.")
"Please come and rest. Make yourself at home."
"May God be praised."
"What is the news?"
"The news, by God's will, is good."

The actions described here follow patterns. They are repeated every time a stranger approaches a Bedouin camp and is invited to be a guest.

Reproduced by permission from: Marion Brady and Howard Brady, *Idea and Action in World Cultures*. Englewood Cliffs, N.J.: Prentice-Hall, 1977, pp. 16-19.

You will recall that the textbook's assertion is that certain behavior patterns can be found in a culture. My note taking, then, should involve looking for evidence to support this assertion. Here they are:

The Bedouins:

1.   wear certain clothes (red head cloth with rope, etc.).
2.   wear hair certain way (long and braided).
3.   ride camel a certain way (center of camel's hump).
4.   approach tent a certain way (zig-zag and toward open side).

If a teacher asked me for evidence of cultural behavior patterns, I could refer to the above notes for examples.

Studying Literature

You will probably study literature courses in school and college. How should you study poems, short stories, novels, and other literary forms? As an English major at Harvard, I found the following two skills especially useful.

Skill 35.   Attend to the "literary" aspects of literature.

When I read novels for pleasure (I am addicted to spy novels), I read them primarily for the story they tell. However, the *literary style* of these novels also has an effect on me. For example, the spy novels of Ian Fleming (the creator of James Bond, Agent 007) appeal to me for their sense of adventure, fast-paced action, exotic locales, and totally evil characters. The novels of John LeCarré (*The Spy Who Came in From the Cold, Tinker, Tailor, Soldier, Spy)* appeal to me for quite different reasons. LeCarré emphasizes mood, psychological conflict, and manifestations of character in desperate situations. Both Fleming and LeCarré tell stories, but *how* they tell them is quite different.

You should realize that the emphasis in literature courses is on how the story is told — no matter whether the story is a novel, a poem, or a short story. This means that you should orient your study to the literary aspects of your literature assignments. What is it that makes them "literature"?

I recommend that you keep a list of *literary aspects* by your side as you read a literature assignment. After reading the assignment, take notes on how the author handles each literary aspect. You can make these notes right after reading a poem or other brief work. In the case of novels, you might take notes after reading each chapter.

The literary aspects that teachers most often focus on are: point of view, recurrent themes, character development, and use of literary devices.

1. *Point of view.* How does the author come across in his or her literary work? Is the author detached or is he emotionally involved in the story he is telling? Is the author sarcastic, sad, optimistic, alienated? For example, my point of view is an intent to communicate directly with the reader. I express this intent by such devices as writing in the first person and recounting personal experiences. There is also a persuasive element in my point of view. I am trying to persuade you that study skills work. I am not indifferent about them. (Indifference would reflect another point of view.)

It takes practice to learn how to detect an author's point of view. Try to "hear" the author's voice as you read, and think about what the author's voice tells you about him or her. To understand what I mean, consider the conversations you have with others. You listen not only to what they say, but *how* they say it. Are they excited, unhappy, argumentative, forceful, hesitant? All of these are "point of view" indicators that you can detect from someone's conversation.

In addition to identifying an author's point of view, you should also take notes on the author's methods for getting his or her point across. For example, how do I persuade you of the importance of the study skills in this book? One method is to list each of them in boldface type; this makes the skills appear authoritative. With respect to great literary works, their authors have the gift of creating sympathy in the reader for their cast of characters. You should attend to methods that the author uses to create sympathy for a character, just as you should also try to detect the author's own attitude — his or her own point of view — toward the character.

2. *Recurrent themes.* Literary works develop certain themes. As you read, identify these themes and jot them down. Examples of literary themes are: the power of nature, human greed, the corrupting influence of power, and the foibles of "polite" society. In addition to identifying themes, you should make notes on the author's insights about them. For example, some of the themes in *The Grapes of Wrath* are adversity, family relationships, and man's inhumanity to man. One of Steinbeck's major insights concerning these themes is how strong family ties and love can help people to cope with terrible adversities.

3. *Character development.* The portrayal of heroes and heroines is a major focus of most novels. As you read a novel, you should take note of who the major characters are. Also, I recommend that you make a few notes at the end of each chapter on how each major character was portrayed in that chapter. Pay special attention to whether each character changed from the way he or she was portrayed in previous chapters. These notes will prove very useful if you are asked, in a course paper or essay exam, to discuss how particular characters are portrayed and how they change over the time frame of the novel.

4. *Use of literary devices.* Your literature courses will probably include instruction in literary devices used by authors to create certain effects. Poems often make use of similes, metaphors, rhythms (pentameter, free verse, etc.), and forms (ballad, ode, sonnet, etc.). Novels and other prose forms (e.g., novellas, short stories, essays) make use of such devices as irony, symbolism, satire, and interior dialogue. Be on the lookout for such literary devices, and take notes on them.

Skill 36. Read critical reviews of literary works to increase your understanding of literature.

Do you ever read movie reviews before or after seeing a movie? The movie reviewer presents facts and interpretations that increase your understanding and appreciation of the movie. Literary reviewers perform the same function for the reader of literature. If you read the essays and books of these reviewers, you can improve your understanding of the literary works that you are assigned to read. Even more important, you will learn by example how to identify the literary aspects of a piece of literature.

Suppose you are taking a course on Shakespeare's plays and are given the assignment of writing a paper about *Hamlet*. I recommend that you look up "Shakespeare" in the library's catalog. You undoubtedly will find some books that provide a literary analysis of Shakespeare's works. Next, I would select one of these books and look in the book's index under *Hamlet*. The index will refer me to sections of the book that discuss this play.

The procedure described above can be used to get ideas for paper topics, or ideas for a topic that you have already identified. For example, you might contrast different literary critics' interpretations of the motivations of the characters in Hamlet. Reviews often point out themes in a literary work. You may decide to select and analyze some of these themes in your paper.

There is nothing unethical about using literary criticism to aid your studies, as long as you do not engage in plagiarism. (Plagiarism refers to the act of copying someone else's writing and claiming it as your own writing rather than giving credit to the true author.) If you wish to quote a passage from a work of literary criticism in your paper, you should indicate that it is a quote by citing the author, title of the work, publisher, and page on which it appears.

It would be time consuming to track down sources of literary criticism for every literary work you are assigned to read. I would reserve this technique for your most important assignments. Surprisingly, teachers seldom require students to read literary criticism. Yet they often read critical essays and books to prepare their own lectures.

Science and Mathematics Textbooks

I have much sympathy for students who wage a constant struggle to understand science textbooks and mathematics textbooks. I was this type of student in college and in graduate school. Although I understand basic math well, advanced math (calculus and beyond) and physics elude me.

What can you do if you are like me and are required to take courses in mathematics-based subjects? The first step is to realize that you must be prepared to spend a lot of time studying for these courses. There is no way around it. I can recall in graduate school spending an hour or more trying to understand a single page of the statistics textbook. Part of my problem was lack of mathematical ability. But another part of the problem was the textbook. It was poorly written, with many concepts insufficiently explained.

In addition to allocating lots of time, you can make use of the three skills described below. My examples refer to math textbooks, but the skills apply equally well to physics textbooks and to other textbooks that use mathematical concepts and notation.

Skill 37.   Do not skip any section of a math-based textbook that you do not understand.

There is a strong temptation, when reading a mathematics textbook, to skip over paragraphs and equations that you do not understand. You may read on in the hope that the author will explain the points you did not understand. This method usually does not help. Mathematical and scientific subjects tend to follow a logical progression. Each new idea builds upon the ideas that preceded it. Therefore, you are likely to become hopelessly lost if you skip over an idea.

When you encounter a section that you do not understand, it is often more productive to turn *back,* rather than go forward, in your textbook. The usual reason why a passage is difficult is that it presumes prior knowledge that you do not have. You cannot acquire this prior knowledge by skipping over the difficult passage to the next section of the textbook. Instead, you need to turn back to learn, or relearn, the concepts presented earlier that are necessary for understanding the section that confused you.

Consider this example. The equation for computing the "mean" of a set of numbers is very important in statistics. The mean is used in many statistical equations. The formula for computing the mean is sometimes given using the following notation (notation may vary from textbook to textbook):

$$M = \frac{\Sigma X}{N}$$

If you cannot make sense of this equation, there is no point in reading ahead in the textbook. It will only get more difficult. The equation will not be explained in any simpler terms, but instead will be used to derive more complex statistical formulas.

Failure to understand the equation presented above probably stems from uncertainty about what each symbol means. These symbols, in all likelihood, were introduced earlier in the textbook. Therefore, you need to turn back to earlier sections of the textbook to refresh your memory about what each symbol in the formula means.

Suppose that re-studying the symbols does not clear up the confusion. Then the problem may be that you do not understand the concept of algebraic equations. If this is true, re-reading previous sections will be of no help, because most authors of statistics textbooks assume that you possess this knowledge. You will need to go back even further. It will be necessary to find a textbook that covers basic algebra and the concept of equations. In fact, many colleges and universities offer courses in "refresher math" for students who are not ready to tackle college-level math. I have even known doctoral students who took such a course to prepare themselves for graduate work in statistics.

Skill 38. Get tutorial help if you need it.

Suppose you get hopelessly bogged down while studying your math or science textbook. No matter how hard you try, it is impossible to follow the author's reasoning. The only solution for this problem is to get help from someone. You might consider asking a classmate or the teacher for help. You should also consider the possibility of hiring a tutor. In college, advanced students are sometimes available as tutors for an hourly fee. Some colleges even have centers that provide tutoring free of charge to students in need.

There is nothing improper about seeking tutorial assistance. As a professor, I have known many graduate students who sought such help as they struggled through courses in statistics and computer programming. My colleagues and I approve of tutors. Our goal — the goal of all teachers — is to help students master their subject areas.

Skill 39. Make sketches to help you solve mathematical problems.

Mathematics or science problems often appear in homework assignments or exams. These problems present a verbal description of a situation and a question that is to be answered. To answer the question, you need to develop a way of representing the elements described in the problem. This process results in an equation, or set of equations, which must be solved without error. Mathematical problem solving is, in fact, quite complicated. The difficulty is compounded by the fact that schools generally do not teach problem-solving skills in a systematic manner.

I have found that making sketches is a good technique for simplifying the problem-solving process. For example, consider the following arithmetic problem:

Which is a better buy: two pens for 38¢ or three pens for 66¢? Figure 9 shows how I would sketch this problem.

Figure 9. Sketch of a Simple Arithmetic Problem

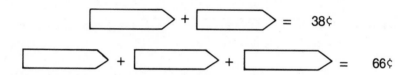

This sketch tells me that I need to find the price of each pen in the sketch. Since the first line has two pens, I need to divide 38¢ by 2 (which is 19¢). Then I divide 66¢ by 3 (because there are 3 pens), and get 22¢. I find that two pens for 38¢ is better because each pen costs 19¢. Three pens for 66¢ is worse because each pen costs 22¢.

Here is a more complicated math problem:

Bill took a bus from his house at an average speed of 18 miles per hour (mph) to see his friend Sam. He spent two hours at Sam's house and then walked home at 3 mph because the bus had stopped running. Bill arrived home exactly 9 hours after he had left for Sam's house. How far is it from Bill's house to Sam's house? Figure 10 shows how this problem can be sketched.

Figure 10. Sketch of a Complex Mathematics Problem

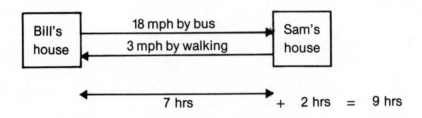

This sketch contains all the information in the problem. It makes clear that the distance travelled by bus and by walking is the same. For those of you who know algebra, the problem can be solved by calling the distance "X" and solving this equation:

$$\frac{X}{18} + \frac{X}{3} = 7$$

If you are like me, you will find that it is much easier to think about a mathematical problem once it is translated into a visual form. (The answer to the problem, by the way, is 18 miles.)

As with any technique, your first efforts at making sketches of mathematical problems may be more trouble than they are worth. With practice, however, you should find that sketches become part of your routine way of solving problems.

5

Writing School Papers

Most students are only required to write short book reports and a few longer papers in junior high and high school. As a consequence, they have trouble when they go to college and later to graduate school. Reports and essays are frequently assigned — as many as five to ten each term. It is not uncommon for students to flunk out of college because they have failed to master the art of writing papers.

This chapter tells you the essential skills for earning good grades on your papers. But I will not minimize the difficulty involved in using these skills. A great deal of time is required to produce a polished paper. Even though I have written eight books and more than 40 articles and professional papers, I still approach writing tasks with reluctance and uncertainty.

I have always wanted to write well. The biggest breakthrough occurred at the end of my first year in graduate school at Berkeley. I had completed an original research project, and my faculty advisor recommended that I write a report of it for publication. He suggested that I write the first draft and he would help me revise it. I wrote the draft and made an appointment to meet with him. It was at this meeting that I achieved new insights into the art of writing.

My faculty advisor is known as a good writer. His style is clear and organized. He started the meeting by suggesting that we revise the first paragraph. I thought this task might take five or ten minutes. To my amazement we spent more than two hours working on this one paragraph. Here was an experienced professor, with many publications to his credit, slaving over a single paragraph. This led to my *first* insight — that academic writing is hard work and requires a large expenditure of time, certainly a lot more time than I ever thought necessary.

What did we do during those two hours? The professor spent a lot of time asking questions that made us think about what we wanted to say and how we wanted to say it. As I recall, some of these questions were: "How can we convince the reader that this study is worth reading?" "What is the main point we want to make in this paragraph?" "Can we say this more effectively?" "Can we assume that the reader will know this term?" "How can we say this more simply?" "Can we improve the transition between these two sentences?"

In trying to answer these questions, my professor sometimes got lost in thought; at other times he drew me into a dialogue, or I volunteered my own questions and ideas. This led me to my *second* insight — that writing is really a process of thinking. The written paragraph is just a condensed expression of a long thought process. In other words, you do not sit down to write. You sit down to think, and in the process, a piece of writing results.

Another thing I observed about the professor's writing style was that he wrote down sentences and phrases in a very tentative way. He gave the impression of sketching in the paragraph. Thus, it was easy for him to scratch out a sentence, move a phrase around, substitute one word for another. Nothing was written down as if it was set in concrete. This led me to my *third* insight — write in a tentative manner and assume that you will make revisions. This makes it much easier to get words on a page. (This principle of writing is similar to the skill of brainstorming, which I will discuss a bit later.)

In case you are interested, here is the final version of the paragraph as it appeared in a journal:

Despite the upsurge of interest in the study of creativity since 1950, there has been relatively little empirical work directed toward the problem of finding techniques to facilitate creative performance. Maltzman's conclusion in 1960 that "most of the work in this important area has been anecdotal or merely hortatory" [p.229] seems equally appropriate today. This is not to say that psychologists and other writers have ignored this

*problem, but rather that the relevant objective information
obtained under controlled conditions is small.*

M. Gall and G. A. Mendelsohn. Effects of facilitating techniques
and subject-experimenter interaction on creative problem solving.
Journal of Personality and Social Psychology. 1967, 5(2),
211-216, p. 211.

There is no way that we could have written this paragraph —
polished, scholarly, concise — in a single draft. It was painstak-
ingly constructed, revision after revision, the product of an
elaborate thinking process.

Now let us examine the problem of writing academic papers
from another perspective. How do teachers go about reading and
grading the papers they assign? I will tell you my approach,
which I think is fairly typical. As a university professor the past
nine years, I have read hundreds of papers at all degree levels —
undergraduate, masters, and doctoral. My approach does not
vary according to degree level, except that I tend to require
higher writing standards from advanced degree students than
from undergraduates.

The first thing I notice is the appearance of the paper. I am
turned off right away if the paper has been typed on cheap
paper, using a faded typing ribbon, and on a typewriter with
defective keys. Reading papers is hard work, and so I get in a
bad mood if the student has made my job more difficult. I feel
much more positive toward students who have handed in nice-
appearing papers. Yes, the appearance of the paper does affect
my evaluation of it.

Typed papers may not be required in junior high and high
school. If not, be sure that the handwriting in your papers is neat
and easy to read. Pen is preferable to pencil. If your handwriting
is poor, I highly recommend you learn how to type so that you
can type all of your school papers.

As I start reading the paper, I first attend to the student's
ideas. Do the ideas make sense? Does he or she have good insights? Are the ideas and insights relevant to the assignment?
Usually I have a good sense of the quality of the student's thinking by the end of the first page of the paper. I have formed a

strong "first impression." I continue reading the rest of the paper, making comments on the margin and checking whether my first impression is still valid. Most of the time my initial judgment is confirmed, but occasionally I need to change it if the student comes on strong in later parts of the paper, or if the student gets off track after the first page or two.

While reading the paper, I also look at the student's spelling, grammar, punctuation, and style. They are not as important as the student's ideas, but they do influence my judgment about the paper's quality. I will overlook a few spelling and punctuation errors, except to circle them. However, if there are many such errors, I get annoyed and penalize the student a half grade or more. For example, a B paper would be given a grade of B- or C+.

I will normally assign a paper with good ideas a grade in the A range (A+, A, A-). A paper that lacks original ideas but manages to get the job done is assigned a grade in the B range. The student is in real trouble, though, if he or she: makes many spelling errors; writes sentences that are impossible to understand; or does not write on the assigned topic or follow directions. Such papers are courting grades in the C, D, and F ranges. I am also ill-disposed toward papers that are handed in late.

To sum up, what you need to do to get A grades on your papers is to hand in papers that follow the teacher's directions, that show evidence of thought, that are technically accurate (spelling, grammar, punctuation) and clear, and that are neat in appearance. Not easy, but for most students an attainable goal.

I know that students sometimes wonder whether teachers actually read their papers. They may believe that the teacher just glances at the first paragraph or two, looks at how many pages the student has written, checks the bibliography to see how many references have been used, and assigns a grade. My experience indicates that teachers usually take written assignments more seriously than this. They read each paper critically and often write comments in the margin and at the end of the paper.

Many different types of papers are assigned in junior high school, high school, college, and graduate school. They range from brief two-page papers to doctoral dissertations that are often a hundred pages long. They vary from interpretive essays to papers reporting on library research or collection of original data. Although these papers differ in length and sources used, the process of writing them is fairly similar. Thus, the following skills should help you in writing most of the papers that you will be assigned in your courses. An exception is creative writing — short stories, poetry, etc. The skills involved in creative writing are not discussed here. These skills are not well understood, and may be less important than natural talent for creative expression.

Skill 40.   Examine good papers written by other students.

One of the best ways to learn a skill is to watch someone who does it well. That is what the apprenticeship system in the trades is all about. For example, novice plumbers learn their trade by working alongside journeyman plumbers, who serve as models. The same principle is used in the professions, also. Young surgeons observe operation after operation performed by highly skilled surgeons. New lawyers serve clerkships so that they can observe experienced judges and criminal lawyers in action.

Unfortunately most of us never get a chance to observe a good writer in action. We could learn a lot by doing so. However, good writers usually isolate themselves while writing to avoid distraction.

If we cannot observe the writing process, at least we can try to observe the product of the writer's efforts. In the case of school papers, they are not usually read by anyone except the teachers who grade them. They are not put out for public display. However, you may be able to obtain examples of highly-graded papers by asking your teachers, classmates, or relatives for any they have on hand.

You can also read published articles in journals relating to the subject you are studying. Many journal articles are written, or co-written, by graduate students, describing research they did as part of their degree requirements. (My article mentioned earlier in this chapter is an example.) These papers reflect the standards that a student must meet for publication of his or her writing. A librarian can help you locate sources of such writing.

Skill 41. *Have a step-by-step plan for writing your paper.*

When given a writing assignment, many of us have a tendency to panic. How do I start? What am I supposed to do? The task is so overwhelming that we have a tendency to avoid it. I know this has been true of me, especially in junior high school when I first started writing papers.

The way to overcome this feeling of panic is to realize that you need to tackle the writing assignment *one step at a time*. And, what are the steps? The following are the basic steps for getting any writing assignment done. I used the steps as a student and I use them now as a professional writer.

Step 1. Identify your topic and the requirements of the writing assignment. This step includes defining a specific, relevant topic and making note of directions you should follow (for example, number of pages, references that should be consulted).

Step 2. Make notes of your ideas. Start making notes as soon as possible, even before you have a clear understanding of the topic or before you have done research on it. Your notes serve as a running diary that you can consult throughout the writing process.

Step 3. Do library research if necessary. Most papers assigned in college and graduate school require you to consult books and journals for facts and ideas. It is important, therefore, that you learn how to use the library as a resource while still in high school, or before.

Step 4. Organize your notes into an outline. It is essential at some point to gather together your personal notes and your library research notes. As you detect patterns and relationships in your notes, fit them together into an outline.

Step 5. Write a first draft of the paper. At this point do not worry about punctuation, grammar, style, and spelling. The emphasis should be on getting your ideas down on paper any way you can.

Step 6. Get "distance" from the first draft, perhaps by having someone read and comment on it. Most of us are so close to our own writing that we cannot judge it critically. We need to get distance from it somehow so that we can detect inconsistencies, undefined terms, weak transitions, and unclear or unsupported statements. These problems should be dealt with in the revision.

Step 7. Revise the paper. If your first draft basically gets across what you want to say, you are ready for the second draft. (Otherwise you will need to write a new "first" draft.) The second draft is your opportunity to start polishing the paper. You can clarify statements, smooth transitions, check spelling, correct punctuation, attend to verb tenses, and so forth. This step, I find, is a lot less difficult than writing the first draft.

Step 8. Repeat Steps 6 and 7. The revision process can be extended depending upon how much time you have available and how good a paper you want to hand in. Someone once said that works of art are never finished, just abandoned. This is also true of school papers. There is always some revision that can be made to improve the paper's quality.

Step 9. Have the paper typed. As I stated above, most teachers, including myself, are influenced in our judgment of a paper by its appearance. You need to set aside time to type the paper, to proofread it for errors, and to make corrections. Otherwise you will need to have the paper typed by someone else, and even this process is time consuming.

Please keep in mind that the steps are not necessarily sequential. You can work on two or three steps at the same time. Or you might leave one step, proceed to the next step, and later return to the one you left. This is perfectly acceptable.

These are the basic steps of writing a paper. Some attention needs to be paid to each step, whether you are writing a two-page paper or a long thesis. The following skills are based on this nine-step plan.

Skill 42. *Allow a substantial amount of time for writing a course paper.*

Most students underestimate the amount of time it takes to write a good course paper. As I stated above, I was amazed to find my faculty advisor spend more than two hours revising the first paragraph of a research report I had drafted.

When I was in college I knew students who boasted how they whipped off a paper in a single evening. Their claims appear to contradict my advice that you should allow a substantial amount of time for writing. However, I have reason to question their claims. For one thing, I have never seen one of these students actually write a paper. Some people have a tendency to exaggerate their accomplishments. They might very well underestimate the time they actually spend. In one sense, though, their claim may be true: the actual paper may have been written in a single long evening. But this does not include the time spent in planning — thinking about the topic, generating ideas, doing library research, making an outline. If these whiz kids added up all the hours in planning and in writing, they would find, I am sure, that they spent a substantial amount of time preparing the paper.

How much time, then, should you figure on spending when writing a paper? As an example, let us consider a typical course paper assigned in college. The professor might ask you to write 10-20 pages; I use 15 pages as an average. I would spend about an hour reading and thinking about the assignment, which is usually described on a handout. Next, I would start scratching notes on binder paper over a period of several days to see what I already know about the topic. If the topic is left for me to choose, I would spend time writing down different topics and selecting the best one. Figure two hours or more for this process.

Library research is next. It is difficult to estimate how much time is needed for this, because it depends so much on the assignment. Therefore, I will use an average based on papers I wrote at Harvard. I recall spending at least three or four evenings in the library tracking down references and reading them. Figuring two hours of such activity each evening, this is a total of eight hours. Organizing my personal notes and library research notes into a working outline of the paper required another hour or so.

Now comes the first draft of the paper. Working from my notes, I figure it took about 40 minutes to write each page of the paper. That's approximately 10 hours. After setting the paper aside for a while, I would return to it, cleaning up style, punctuation, etc. If extensive rewriting was not required, I would figure about 15 minutes per page for this editing process — approximately 4 hours for a 15-page paper. Add another hour or so to write my bibliography in an approved style. Typing the paper takes about a half hour per page. Then I need an hour to proofread it and to correct typo's. So that is about nine hours to type the paper.

The total of all these numbers is as follows:

1 hour	Assignment clarification
2 hours	Thinking and initial planning
8 hours	Library research
1 hour	Make outline
10 hours	First draft
5 hours	Revision and bibliography
9 hours	Typing
36 hours	total

Thirty-six hours to write a 15-page paper. This is a lot of time, but it is a conservative estimate of what is required to write a *good* course paper. Of course, if you know your subject very well, can write fast, and have the paper typed by someone else, you can shave a lot of time from this estimate. Perhaps the paper could be written in 25 hours. That is still a lot of time.

I think a major reason why so many students have a difficult time in college is that they have no idea how much time they need to allocate to their studies, especially to the task of writing course papers. Writing is difficult and time consuming.

Skill 43. Hand in your paper on time.

Most teachers frown on papers that are handed in after the due date. It makes extra work for them. They also do not like listening to "sob" stories and deciding whether they are true. Even if the student says that a crisis occurred at the last minute, the teacher will wonder why the student did not plan better so that the paper was completed before the crisis occurred. Also, teachers are concerned about being fair to all the students who handed in their papers on time. Some of these students may have had a crisis, too, and wrote their papers under pressure with some loss in quality. Why should they be penalized while late students incur no penalty at all? Unless the late student has a good excuse, with supporting evidence, many teachers will penalize him or her by assigning a lower grade. For example, an A- paper might be given a grade of B.

The lesson is clear. Plan your time so you are sure that your paper will be finished by the due date.

Skill 44. Analyze the paper assignment carefully.

The more your know about an assigned paper, the easier it is to write. You need to figure out what the teacher wants you to do. This is not always an easy task because the teacher may not have thought through what he or she expects students to do.

As a professor, I give my students a detailed handout that describes the topic (or choice of topics), the number of pages that should be written, references that should be consulted, points that should be covered, and format (for example, typed and double-spaced). If the teacher has not specified this information, I recommend that you ask him or her to do so.

When I was a college student, I made a point of seeing the professor or professor's assistant if I was unclear about any aspect of the assignment. There is no point in going ahead with the writing process if you are starting off on the wrong track. In fact, the professor or assistant was always willing to clarify the assignment. They knew that if they gave a vague writing assignment, students would hand in vague papers, which are no pleasure to read.

I find that students have two common problems in analyzing a paper assignment. The first problem is figuring out how many pages to write. Suppose the teacher specifies that the paper should be 10 to 15 pages in length. Should you write a paper at the lower limit (10 pages) or at the higher limit (15 pages)? Or should you try to write a longer paper than required — perhaps 20 pages or so — to show the teacher how motivated you are? My view is that you should aim for writing 15 pages. A 10-page paper is just fine, if it is tightly written — substantive and concise. However, unless you are exceptional, you will have a lot of difficulty writing good concise prose. Even professional writers usually write a longer paper, then keep editing it to achieve a concise, tightly-written effect.

I would not recommend writing much more than the teacher's upper limit, either. The teacher may subconsciously resent having to read a longer paper than required by the assignment. Also, if you strain to write a long paper, there is a tendency to pad it with long quotes, excessive detail, and bibliographic references not actually cited in the paper. If the teacher senses that this is what you are doing, he or she may penalize you in grading the paper.

The other problem that plagues students is figuring out what to do if the teacher does not assign a specific topic. For example, the assignment might state, "Select an aspect of Freud's theory of human development and compare it with Jung's theory in a 10-page paper." This assignment is a bit vague. What does the teacher mean by "aspect"? How much of Freud's theory does an "aspect" include? You can get into difficulty if you select too broad or too narrow an aspect of Freud's theory. If too broad, you will not be able to discuss anything in detail within the page allotment. If too narrow, you will not have much to write about.

Here is what I recommend doing when the topic is not assigned. Spend some time thinking of different ideas and jot them down. When you have narrowed down to one or two topics, see the teacher. (If you are in college, you may need to see the professor's assistant.) Ask for his or her opinion on your topics. This feedback will help you greatly in defining your topic and will give you the confidence to proceed with the writing process.

Skill 45.   *State your paper topic as an intellectual task you will accomplish.*

Many students get off to a bad start by trying to write about a "thing." For example: the Cuban missile crisis; the Battle at Gettysburg; the concept of romantic love in the Middle Ages; geothermal energy. A student might start his paper with the statement, "The purpose of this paper is to discuss the Cuban missile crisis in John Kennedy's administration." The problem with a statement like this is that it poses no interesting intellectual task. Here are some examples of intellectual tasks:

1.   Make *comparisons* between _____.

2.   Show the *development* of a(n) _____.

3.   *Evaluate* and criticize _____.

4. *Analyze* why _____ happened or why someone did a certain thing.

5. Explore the *consequences* of _____ .

Using this approach, the student could define the topic as "A comparison of John Kennedy's handling of the Cuban missile crisis at three different stages of the crisis."

To show you how this approach works, let us consider the topic "solar energy." Here is how you can develop five intellectually interesting topics using the list above:

1. Compare the benefits of solar energy and wind-powered energy as alternatives to nuclear power plants.

2. Show how solar energy was developed as an energy alternative by government policy-makers during the past decade.

3. Evaluate whether government policy-makers are giving solar energy sufficient emphasis within its overall energy program.

4. Analyze why certain communities decided to exploit their solar energy sources whereas other communities ignored them.

5. Explore the economic consequences of creating incentives for home use of solar energy devices.

Even though I know very little about solar energy, I had no difficulty defining five topics using the list of intellectual tasks presented above. Another advantage of stating topics this way is that they provide immediate direction to the type of library research and paper organization that will be required.

The list of five tasks can be elaborated by combining two or more tasks into a single task. For example: "The purpose of this paper is to *compare* the likely pattern of development of solar energy and wind-powered energy over the next five years, and to *evaluate* which of these two energy sources is most ready for commercial exploitation."

Skill 46. State the purpose of the paper in the first paragraph.

The first paragraph of a school paper is often the most difficult to write. If you have trouble getting started, here is a simple technique you can use. Write a statement beginning with the phrase, "The purpose of this paper is to (demonstrate, examine, analyze)..." Remember to state the purpose as an intellectual task to be accomplished (see Skill 45). Next, write a few sentences that further describe the purpose or build a case for its importance. Use these sentences to start the paragraph and conclude with your "The purpose ..." sentence.

As an example, I wrote a possible opening paragraph for the first chapter of this book using these procedures:

Many students think that going to school is a matter of "soaking in" new knowledge. If they sit through enough classes, they'll earn a diploma. These students fail to realize that school requires a great deal of independent study and that they must study actively if they are to be successful. The purpose of this book is to show you the most important techniques for being an active learner in high school, college, or graduate school.

This is not a great first paragraph, but it is all right for a first draft. It serves the important purpose of getting me started on drafting the chapter.

Skill 47. Use brainstorming to develop ideas for your paper.

Brainstorming is a proven technique that can be used in many areas of work. It is especially useful in the writing process. I have come to rely increasingly over the years on brainstorming to aid my thinking.

Brainstorming principles were first systematically developed in advertising. Advertising requires a constant stream of creativity. New slogans, names for products, and jingles are continually needed. In the 1930's Thomas Gordon, an advertising executive, proposed that brainstorming be used to satisfy this constant need for creativity. He showed that brainstorming is a three-step process. The *first* step is to define a problem to be solved. In the case of advertising, the problem might be to find a name for a new product.

The *second* step in brainstorming is to think of as many solutions to the problem as you can. This is done by suspending criticism. Just generate solutions without regard to their merit or appropriateness. If you criticize each idea you generate, you will impede the creative flow of ideas. Instead, you should nourish the flow of ideas. You want to generate as many ideas as possible.

You also want to encourage "piggybacking" at this stage of brainstorming. Piggybacking means that you let one idea build upon another. For example, if a small group of people are brainstorming, one person might say something that sparks a related idea in me. So I might say, "Let me piggyback on that idea. We could name the new product _____ ."

To show you how this second step of brainstorming works, I am going to write down names as they come to me for labeling a new soap. Here goes:

> Soap — Clean — Wash — Clean Bill — Fresh Spring —
> Rain Clean — Pure — Skin Glow — Skin Clean — Fresh
> Scent — Skin Fresh — Fresh and Clean — Dirt Away —
> Suds — Soapy Suds — Scrub — Fresh Scrub — Rub It Off
> — Rub and Scrub — Soapy Scrub — Scrub n' Glow

Some of these names, which I generated in just a few minutes, are silly. In fact, they seemed silly the moment I thought of them. But since this stage of brainstorming involves the *total* suspension of judgment, I wrote down all my ideas. You will note that some of the names are similar to or build upon names that I had just generated. This is piggybacking in action.

Once you have generated a bunch of ideas, while withholding criticism, you are ready for the *third* stage of brainstorming. In this stage you use critical judgment to select the best idea among the many that you have generated. Critical judgment occurs in two phases. In the first phase, you develop criteria for selecting the best of your ideas. Given the task of naming a new soap (see above), some criteria might be:

1. The name cannot be the same as, or sound similar to, the name of any cleaning product currently on the market.

2. The name must suggest, directly or indirectly, that this is a cleaning product.

3. The name must not sound silly; it should appeal to the sophisticated shopper, for whom it is intended.

4. The name cannot be more than 10 letters long.

5. The name should form easy rhymes.

Note that you can even use brainstorming (second step) to generate criteria; then apply critical judgment (third step) to decide which criteria you will actually use.

After deciding on criteria, you can go to the next phase, which involves using the criteria to select the best solution to the problem. At this point, you can be as critical as you want about the solutions you brainstormed in phase two.

Brainstorming is often done by small groups of people working to solve a given problem. However, researchers have found that an individual working alone usually does just as well — and sometimes better — than a group.

Brainstorming procedures can be used throughout the entire writing process. For example, to create an outline for a paper, I will go through my notes and whenever I spot anything that looks like a possible heading, I jot it down. I do not worry at this point whether it is important enough to be a heading or whether it should be a main heading or subheading. I usually generate more headings than I will actually use. After generating a list of headings, I then become more critical. I prune the list and then decide whether the remaining items should be main headings or subheadings.

In writing the first draft of a paper, I suspend self-criticism as much as possible. I just want to get words on paper. If I get too critical at this point, my writing becomes stalled. I do not worry about the length of my sentences and paragraphs, or about spelling and grammar. If I write something that strikes me as awkward or unclear, I either may rewrite it or just leave it as it is, knowing I can come back to it in my second draft. If I get stuck on a point or lack information to write a particular paragraph, I do not worry about it. I just move to the next point or paragraph so I can keep the creative flow going.

Brainstorming is also useful during the revision process. If I am concerned about which word to use in a sentence, I think of several alternatives and then select the one that seems best. Similarly, to get a title for the paper, I generate titles for a while, then sit back to evelute which, if any, is suitable.

Basically, brainstorming is a process of alternately suspending and applying critical judgment. The suspension of judgment is important because it frees the creative process and prevents you from developing "writer's block." Critical judgment is also important, because it enables you to separate the good from the bad, the relevant from the irrelevant.

Skill 48.   *Use a conversational tone when you write the first draft of a school paper.*

Like many students, I used to try writing in a scholarly, academic style. This gets students into a lot of difficulty because it is not a natural style of communication. If we try to achieve a scholarly tone, our prose is likely to be pretentious, stilted, artificial. Even you may not understand what you write.

We see a similar phenomenon in children's art. Before children enter school, their drawings are imaginative and original. After having been in school a while, many children produce art that is routine and uninteresting. This is because school children are instructed to imitate models of what is correct and proper, rather than to do what comes naturally.

I have always found it fascinating that most students have no difficulty writing personal letters. The letters just seem to flow. Why is this? The reason is that we let ourselves be natural when we write personal letters. In writing school papers, though, we try to be someone we are not. That gets us into trouble.

My recommendation is that you remember to just be yourself when you write the first draft of a school paper. Write in a conversational tone; use simple words and sentences; state your ideas directly without a long preamble; use the word "I" if you wish. Believe me, this will make it much easier to get words onto paper.

Once you have written your paper in conversational style, you can revise it to convey a more formal tone. For example, if your teacher requires you to write in the third person, it is a simple enough matter to change any "I" statements you have made. Consider the sentence, "I don't agree with the view that the great white whale in *Moby Dick* is supposed to stand for the evil that's in the world." It can be changed to this third person-statement and made more formal with a few changes: "The view that the great white whale in *Moby Dick* personifies worldly evil is debatable."

My point is that it is easier to achieve a formal tone if you do not try to do it in the first draft of your paper. Allow your first draft to be natural and expressive. Concentrate on what you are trying to say, not on how to say it.

Skill 49. Write from an outline.

It is very difficult to write a well-organized paper if you do not first make an outline. By this I do not mean a fancy outline with all sorts of headings and with an elaborate numbering system (I.1.a, I.1.b, and so on). My outlines are much rougher than this. I keep each heading and idea as brief as possible until I achieve an overall outline that I can live with.

I put short notes in the margin or beside the headings to remind me of points I want to be sure to make. At this first stage, then, I want a brief outline that shows me the overall organization of the paper. It should show all the major points that I wish to make and the order in which I will make them. (See Skill 47 on the use of brainstorming to create outlines.)

When the main outline is done, I make another set of mini-outlines as I write the paper. For example, the first heading of my outline is usually "Introduction." I might have one or two brief notes next to this heading. When it actually comes time to write the introduction, I further outline it and write that section of the paper from my outline. I then outline the next section, write it, and so on. For example, in writing this chapter I reviewed my notes and drafted an outline that consisted of a list of the study skills presented here, each described in just a few words. I kept re-arranging the list until I had the skills arranged in the order that I wished to write about them. Then, I outlined what I wanted to say about each skill before sitting down to write about it. Because I am so familiar with the skills, my mini-outlines generally consist of very brief sentences and phrases. I number these sentences and phrases to remind me of the order in which I wish to elaborate on them.

Creating an outline may delay you a bit from starting on the first draft of your paper. However, you will save time later on, because the outline speeds up writing the first draft and reduces the amount of revision necessary.

Skill 50.   Consult the librarian for help when doing library research.

You will need to use the library for many of the papers assigned in school. The process of using the library to collect facts and ideas relating to your topic is called *library research.* Unfortunately, few of us are taught systematically how to do library research. This certainly was true of me at Harvard. I knew how to use the library catalog and how to locate a book or journal on the library shelves by its call number. But I knew almost nothing about the special aids that are available to facilitate library research.

It is helpful to think about library resources at three levels. The first level is the *bibliographic index.* This is the level that students know least about. Bibliographic indexes are designed to help you identify what has been written about a particular topic. For example, *Psychological Abstracts,* which is published monthly and cumulated annually, enables you to identify all journal articles that have been written on a particular psychological topic within a certain period of time. For example, if you wanted to review research on dreams, you could quickly obtain a list of relevant research articles by consulting *Psychological Abstracts.* Each major academic discipline has a similar indexing service to help you locate literature relating to a particular topic.

Other types of bibliographic index are available, too. For example, *National Newspaper Index* is an index to newspaper articles that have been written about particular topics. *Magazine Index* is an index to more than 370 popular magazines. These few examples illustrate the great range of bibliographic indexes that are available for specialized needs. Many of these indexes are in catalog format, but increasingly they are being computerized. I have had a few computer searches made for literature on a particular topic. These searches are remarkably quick and comprehensive, but they do cost money.

How do you learn about bibliographic indexes that would help you write your paper? What I have found most helpful over the years is to ask a librarian for assistance. I used to think that librarians only checked out books and sent overdue notices. However, a good public library or college library will have librarians who specialize in different academic disciplines. If I want information relating to a topic in my own disciplines (psychology and education), I will go to the Education-

Psychology section of our library to ask one of the librarians located there for help. I am always impressed by how knowledgeable and helpful they are.

One requirement for using bibliographic indexes is the need to describe your topic in precise terms. You must define the topic using a "descriptor" that is included in the index. For example, if you were interested in locating references on Freud's theory of dreams, you might need to try various descriptors such as "Freud," "psychoanalytic theory," and "dreams." Some descriptors might not be listed in the index; you need to keep trying until you hit paydirt. If you are having difficulty finding a descriptor that works, I recommend asking the librarian for assistance.

Suppose that the descriptor is included in the bibliographic index that you have consulted. Beneath the descriptor will be a list of references that have been published on that topic over a certain period of time. Each reference will contain the author(s), title, date of publication, publisher (if a book) or journal and page numbers (if a journal). Some bibliographic indexes also include a brief summary of the reference's content.

Bibliographic indexes are the first level of library resources. The second level is *secondary sources*. These are books and articles that review, summarize, or discuss other sources of information. I find that secondary sources are extremely helpful in doing library research on a topic. For example, if I am interested in research studies that have been done to test Freud's theory of dreams, I would consult a bibliographic aid to determine whether someone has done a recent review of these studies. If a review is available, it will be the first thing I will read. The review will suggest how the research can be organized in terms of themes or underlying problems being investigated; and it provides a bibliography of the actual research articles.

Encyclopedia articles and review articles in journals or books are a major secondary source. Textbooks, too, are another type of secondary source because they are compilations of what is known about a particular subject. Many textbooks include at the end of each chapter a bibliography that might help to guide your library research.

The third level of bibliographic resources is *primary sources.* (See Skill 34 for ideas on how to take notes on primary sources.) These are original documents written by the person or persons who actually witnessed an event, conducted a research study, or created a piece of literature. Research reports, eyewitness accounts, correspondence, diaries, novels, and poetry are examples of primary sources. President Nixon's resignation speech would be a primary source; Woodward and Bernstein's account of events leading up to the resignation would be a secondary source. Shakespeare's *Hamlet* would be a primary source; a literary critic's interpretation of it would be a secondary source.

You might think of primary sources as being close in time and place to the phenomena you are studying. Secondary sources are more removed in time and place from the phenomena.

In doing library research, you will need to decide the extent to which you will consult secondary sources versus primary sources. In a way, secondary sources are more useful because they are comprehensive and contain interpretations. On the other hand, primary sources are the "real stuff" and so they provide a better basis for developing original insights into the phenomena being studied. They are often time consuming to track down and read, though. What I generally did in writing school papers was to rely extensively on secondary sources for ideas and information. I also tried to read at least one or two of the most pertinent primary sources. I made certain to indicate in my paper that I had read these primary sources by quoting from them or discussing them knowledgeably. This strategy, in addition to enhancing my learning, set off my course papers from the papers of students who relied exclusively on secondary sources.

Primary source documents are sometimes difficult to locate in a library. They may be published in obscure journals, government publications, pamphlets, or other non-book formats. Again, I recommend that you ask a librarian for assistance. They are trained to locate these items. I also rely on librarians for difficult-to-find information that I need when writing an article or book. For example, I recently needed to know the average school district expenditure for curriculum materials as a percentage of total school district expenditures. The few resources I had available did not contain this information, and I did not know where else to look. I asked a librarian for assistance, and she was able to locate several useful primary sources that I did not know existed.

Skill 51.   Make copies of your reference sources.

Photocopy machines were not available when I was a student at Harvard. Therefore, whenever I did library research, I had to make extensive notes on reference sources that could not be checked out from the library (for example, bound volumes of journals and reference books). Note taking is very time consuming, especially if you copy sections of the text so that you can use them later as direct quotes in your paper.

This time-consuming procedure is no longer necessary. College libraries and public libraries usually have conveniently-located photocopy machines on which you can make a copy of any printed material. If the machines are not available or broken, you usually can check out the materials for an hour or two and have them photocopied at a copy shop.

Because of the easy availability of photocopy machines, I almost never take notes any more on reference sources that I need for my writings. Instead, I make a copy of anything that cannot be checked out from the library for a sufficient period of time. When I have made the copy, I am free to underline relevant sections of it and to make notes in the margin.

Some students are reluctant to use the photocopy machine because of the expense involved. My opinion is that the expense is well worth it compared to the time and effort required to make notes. Also, there is the possibility that your notes will be incomplete and you will need to spend a lot of time returning to the library to make more notes. This has happened to me on a number of occasions.

Skill 52. Include ideas from library sources in your paper.

Let us assume that you have spent a lot of time doing library research for your paper. It is only reasonable to want your teacher to know that you made this effort. You need to include your library research findings in the paper in a way that is obvious and clear. At the same time you should avoid needless showing off. How can you do this?

My approach is to blend in the references with my own writing. For example, I might write a statement this way:

Some of Freud's early followers (Jung, 1934; Adler, 1936) later came to question his theory of dreams.

Or I might use a footnote system:

Some of Freud's early followers later came to question his theory of dreams.[1]

I recommend that all of the footnotes be placed together on a separate page at the end of the paper. This way all of the footnotes can be seen easily by the teacher. Another approach is to put each footnote at the bottom of the page where it is referred to in the text. The disadvantage of the second approach is that bottom-of-the-page footnotes are difficult to type.

I strongly recommend against extensive use of direct quotes in your papers. Some students use two or three quotes per page, and some are long (anything more than four or five lines is long). This gives the teacher the impression that you are "padding" the paper and that you have not really digested what your sources have said. It is much better to paraphrase your source, as in the following:

Some of Freud's early followers (Jung, 1934; Adler, 1936) later came to question his theory of dreams. For example, Jung argued that Freud completely overlooked the mythic component that is present in many dreams (Jung, 1934, page 76).

The page citation indicates that you can document your assertion, and your paraphrase indicates that you understand the source that you have cited.

Should you include in your paper some of the facts that the teacher presented in class? I recommend this if it is done tastefully. Citing the teacher only for the purpose of flattery can have a backlash effect. I recommend that you make no more than one or two direct references to the teacher's views in a paper. They should be brief and to the point.

Skill 53. Keep track of bibliographic information on references you cite.

In writing your paper, you should present the facts and evidence uncovered in your library research. You should also cite the sources from which they were obtained. The sources of direct quotes also need to be cited. Therefore, you need to record information on your bibliographic sources as you do your library research.

Keeping track of the source of each bibliographic citation is very important. It may be difficult later on to remember where you obtained a particular piece of information or quote. Also, you need a complete reference so that you can give a proper citation if you decide to include the information in your paper.

Problems can be avoided by making a complete bibliographic citation for each source that you find in the library. For a magazine or journal article, you should include the author, title, name of the journal or magazine, volume number, date, and page numbers. For a book, be sure to include the name of the author, title, publisher, edition number if any, and latest copyright date. Below is an example of a typical magazine citation and a typical book citation.

Howe, Irving. "James Baldwin: At Ease in
Apocalypse." *Harper's,* Sept. 1968, pp. 92-100.

Bolles, Richard N. *What Color Is Your Parachute?*
Berkeley, Calif.: Ten Speed Press, 1982.

Be sure to make a note of page numbers for any material that you intend to quote directly in your paper. It is also a good idea to write down the library catalog number of the volume from which you copied a journal article or section. This will come in handy in case you need to retrieve the volume again at a later date.

Skill 54.   Start writing while still doing library research.

I may have given the impression that writing a paper occurs in a series of steps: define a topic, do library research, make an outline, write a first draft. In fact, these steps overlap each other. This is particularly true when you are doing library research. How do you know when you have done enough library research? How do you know you have tracked down the right references? To answer these questions, you need to start outlining your paper as soon as you have a small set of notes to work from. The outline can show you where the gaps in your library research are.

Sometimes it is good to proceed to the next step — writing the first draft — and continue doing library research on an "as needed" basis. I remember times when I was writing a first draft and discovered that my notes and reference sources were insufficient for me to write knowledgeably about the topic. Consequently I made another trip to the library to do more research.

A famous historian, Edward Carr, described well this process of alternating between library research and writing drafts of the paper:

Laymen ... sometimes ask me how the historian goes to work when he writes history. The commonest assumption appears to be that the historian divides his work into two sharply distinguishable phases or periods. First, he spends a long preliminary period reading his sources and filling his notebooks with facts; then, when this is over, he puts away his sources, takes out his notebooks, and writes his book from beginning to end. This is to me an unconvincing and unplausible picture. For myself, as soon as I have got going on a few of what I take to be the capital sources, the itch becomes too strong and I begin to write — not necessarily at the beginning, but somewhere, anywhere. Thereafter, reading and writing go on simultaneously. The writing is added to, subtracted from, re-shaped, cancelled, as I go on reading. The reading is guided and directed and made fruitful by the writing: the more I write, the more I know what I am looking for, the better I understand the significance and relevance of what I find.

E. H. Carr. *What Is History?* New York: Random House, 1967, pp. 32-33.

I do not think that you need to use as sophisticated a process as that described by Carr in writing a typical course paper. Extensive library research and documentation are not necessary. However, at some point you may need to write a long paper — for example, a senior honors thesis in college. These long assignments often require extensive library research.

Skill 55. Get distance from your first draft by asking yourself questions about it.

The best technique for getting objective feedback on your writing, I think, is to have someone critique it (see Skill 56). However, there are some steps you can take on your own. As you read through the draft of your paper, keep asking yourself these questions:

1. Will this sentence or paragraph be clear to the reader? Did I use any vague or imprecise words? Did I use terms that should be defined? Can I give an example to illustrate what I mean?

2. Is this sentence or paragraph relevant to my topic and arguments?

3. Does this sentence or paragraph follow meaningfully from the previous one?

4. Can this sentence or paragraph be stated more concisely?

The readability of a paper is improved whenever you can state the same idea in fewer words. For example, the first draft of Question 4 was, "Can this sentence or paragraph be stated in a more precise way?" In the final draft, I was able to shorten the sentence by three words ("more concisely" versus "in a more precise way").

The technique of asking self-critical questions will only work if you are willing to make changes in your paper. You are not likely to make changes if you wait until the last minute. Obviously you need to set aside a block of time specifically for the revision process.

Suppose you ask one of the above questions, and your answer is "No." When this happens to me, I back away from the writing task. I ask myself, "What am I trying to say in this sentence?" Basically, I talk it out to myself. It is much easier to *talk* it out than to *write* it out. When the idea becomes clear in my mind, I then write it down.

Skill 56. Ask another person to review your first draft.

Once you have written a first draft of your paper, then what? When I was a student, I used to just stare at my first draft. It looked cast in concrete. I knew it was not good, but I could not figure out how to improve it. The problem was that I was too close to my writing. I could not get enough "distance" from it to be able to judge its strengths and weaknesses objectively.

I am not the only person with this problem. Even professional writers have difficulty being objective about revising their work. The solution to the problem is obvious, once you think about it. Publishers employ editors and consultants who work with authors to improve their writing. Before a book is published, it is sent for review to consultants who are experts in the field covered in the manuscript. Each consultant writes a detailed critique. The critiques note strengths and specific weaknesses of the manuscript. As an author of eight textbooks, I have received a number of these critiques and found them very helpful.

After the content of the manuscript has been revised based on the consultants' critiques, it is sent to the publisher again. The publisher then sends it to a person known as a copy editor, who reviews it line-by-line for clarity, consistency, style, punctuation, and grammar. Copy editors assigned to my manuscripts have marked them extensively, making many worthwhile revisions in them. Also, they noted sentences and paragraphs that were unclear or inconsistent with something I wrote elsewhere in the manuscript. These notes (called "queries") are items that the copy editor cannot correct. They are sent to the author with a request to make the necessary revisions.

In a similar manner, you can improve the first draft of your paper by having someone do a critique of it. Unfortunately, I did not know of this technique in college so my efforts at revision were usually ineffective. At some point in graduate school, though, it occurred to me to ask one of my classmates to critique drafts of papers that I wrote for doctoral seminars. Since graduate school, I have never submitted a paper or book for publication without first having one or two colleagues critique it.

I strongly recommend that you ask someone you know to give you critical feedback on first drafts of your school papers. The critique should cover both content and style. Perhaps your parents or a school friend can do this for you.

Skill 57. *Work on technical aspects of your paper in the second draft.*

As I indicated earlier in the chapter, most school papers should be written in at least two drafts. You should focus in the first draft on what you want to say. You will have your hands full converting your notes and outline into a flow of sentences and paragraphs. It may take you one or two drafts before all your facts and ideas are clearly and logically stated in the paper. Then you are ready to work on the technical details of the paper.

In using the term "technical details," I am referring to such matters as grammar, spelling, punctuation, footnotes, and bibliography. If these details are handled sloppily, your teacher may lower the grade on your paper. I have read hundreds of papers written by students. The following are the most common technical weaknesses that I have come across.

1. *Incomplete sentences.* For example, "Japanese society in the sixteenth century was characterized by three elements. A feudal hierarchy, ancestor worship, and constant war." The problem can be corrected by making one long sentence with a colon: "Japanese society in the sixteenth century was characterized by three elements: a feudal hierarchy, ancestor worship, and constant war." There are situations where incomplete sentences can be used effectively, but I recommend you not try using them unless you are in firm control of your writing style.

2. *Spelling errors.* A few students have a chronic spelling problem, but most of us just trip over the more difficult words. Words that sound similar, but are spelled differently, are especially difficult, for example, "affect" and "effect," "affective" and "effective," "principal" and "principle," "stationary" and "stationery."

3. *Long paragraphs.* A short paragraph of two or three sentences is generally more acceptable than a long paragraph. I sometimes read paragraphs in student papers that are a page or more. Long paragraphs give the teacher the impression that the student is disorganized. I doubt there is ever a need to have a paragraph more than 10 typed lines, or 6-7 sentences, long.

4. *Wrong choice of words.* Students sometimes think that they can impress a teacher by using an academic-sounding word. For example, "Karl Marx averred that ..." instead of the more direct form, "Karl Marx stated that ..."; "If you desire to ..." instead of the simpler "If you wish to ..."; "proclination" instead of "tendency." I generally recommend against using "two-dollar" words unless they are needed.

5. *Peculiar sentence construction.* It is easy to fall all over yourself trying to harness an idea to a sentence. I suggest that you read your writing quietly to yourself to see if it sounds right. If a sentence does not sound right, the cause is normally that it is too long or grammatically complex. The remedy is to break a long sentence into two shorter sentences, or to use a simpler grammatical structure. For example, consider this sentence: "In contrast to Nicholson, Adams advocated a pay-as-you-go taxation approach to the financing of large-scale capital expenditures,

such as the construction of sewage treatment plants and city halls, whereas he advocated a bonding approach to the development of public services such as veterans' home loans and displaced homemaker programs.''

So much is going on in this sentence that it is impossible to keep straight all of the positions held by Nicholson and Adams. Here is an example of how the preceding sentence might be simplified: "Nicholson and Adams differed in their approach to financing governmental projects. Consider the financing of large-scale capital projects, such as the construction of sewage treatment plants and city halls. Adams advocated a pay-as-you-go taxation approach, whereas Nicholson favored bonding. Also consider the financing of public services such as veterans' home loans and displaced homemaker programs. Adams favored bonding to finance these services, but Nicholson favored taxation. Thus, they had entirely different views of how taxation and bonding could be used to finance government.'' The second version is a bit longer, but much clearer.

6. *Vague referents.* Avoid using "this" and "that" as nouns, because it is usually difficult to determine what the "this" or "that" refers to. Consider this example: "Charles Dickens' dislike of the legal profession was reflected in several themes that dominated his major novels. This is important to developing an understanding of his novels' reception by the Victorian reading public." What does "this" refer to? Dickens' dislike of the legal profession? The reflection of this dislike in his novels? The themes that dominated his novels? The best way to avoid this type of ambiguity is to not use "this," "that," or "it" as referents.

Another type of vague referent is known as a "dangling participle." Here is an example: "Having noticed the inconsistencies in the data from the two studies, a new theory had to be developed." The person who did the observing is not indicated. If you start a sentence with a participial clause (e.g., "Having observed . . ."), you must start the second part of the sentence with the person or thing that is the subject of the participial clause. The sentence used as an example above might be rewritten: "Having noticed the inconsistencies in the data from the two studies, Johnson concluded that a new theory was needed.''

7. *Choice of tense and tense agreement.* Choice of the correct tense is sometimes difficult in writing school papers. The subjunctive tense is especially difficult. The best advice I can give about the proper use of the subjunctive is to read sentences containing them quietly to yourself. Keep trying different tenses until you hit one that sounds right. For example, "If Napoleon would have done ..." sounds odd whereas "If Napoleon had done ..." sounds natural.

Another problem is deciding what tense to use in different situations. For example, which is correct: "In his last published novel, Salinger *expresses* the view ..." or "In his last published novel, Salinger *expressed* the view ..."? Also, which is correct: "The data indicated that males *earn* higher scores than females on a mathematics test" or "The data indicated that males *earned* higher scores than females on a mathematics test"?

The correct rule is to use the past tense whenever the event being referred to has already occurred. Thus, I would opt for "expressed" in the first example above. The other rule is to use the present tense to refer to research findings and to facts that are still true today. Thus, I would use "earn" in the second example above. Another application of these two rules is found in the following sentence: "In 1900 most U.S. cities were rapidly gaining population, whereas at the present time they are losing population".

Skill 58.   *Use headings in your paper.*

The use of headings is a simple way to improve the organization and appearance of your paper. Surprisingly few students make use of them. If you can make a habit of incorporating headings into your papers, you will have an edge over other students' papers. Three types of heading are commonly used.

Center headings. The first type is the center heading. These are headings that are positioned at the center of the page. They introduce major topics around which the paper is organized. Generally you will have no more than one center heading for every two or three pages of your paper. These headings should be quite brief, as in these examples: Introduction; Northern Liberals' View of Slavery; Southern Liberals' View of Slavery; Western Liberals' View of Slavery; Comparison of Views. Center headings should occur no more than each two to five pages of a paper.

Side headings. This type of heading usually introduces subtopics that are to be discussed under a center heading. They are most useful when, under a center heading, you have a long discussion treating several distinct topics. Side headings can be used without center headings, though, as I have done in this chapter. Each bold-faced label naming a skill (for example, "Skill 58. Use headings in your paper.") is a side heading. There usually should not be more than one side heading per page.

Paragraph headings. These are headings that introduce the topic discussed in a particular paragraph or a series of paragraphs. The paragraph headings used here ("Center headings," "Side headings," "Paragraph headings") illustrate what they look like. Paragraph headings generally are not used unless they follow a center or side heading. They are useful when you have a lot of information that needs to be organized for the reader.

Try making use of headings in the next school paper you write. I believe you will find that headings improve its clarity and appearance, which should favorably impress the teacher.

Skill 59. Leave space on your first draft for revisions, or put them on separate sheets of paper.

Minor revisions, such as correction of spelling errors and punctuation, can be made right on your first draft. Brief changes in phrasing can be made in the margins. You can also do some rewriting on the first draft if you use wide-rule paper. (Packages of binder paper are usually labeled "wide rule," "college rule," or "narrow rule." "College rule" is the same as "narrow rule.") If your handwriting is not too large, there will be space to write your first draft and a revision on the same line. Some students write their first draft double-spaced, meaning that every other line is left blank. If this method works for you, use it. A double-spaced draft does not work for me because I lose my sense of how long my paragraphs are.

Another method I use to make revising easier is to leave extra-wide margins on the left side of the paper. Wide margins also make it easier for reviewers to write comments next to the sentences and paragraphs to which they pertain.

It is not always possible to make revisions on the first draft. The revision may be too lengthy, or you may be unsure about how to phrase the revision. In these situations it is best to write your revisions on a separate sheet of paper. This gives you all the space you need to try out different phrasings until you write one that satisfies you.

There are two methods for integrating revisions that are on separate sheets of paper with your first draft. One method is to cut-and-paste or cut-and-tape each revision into the draft. I do not favor this method because it is time consuming. I favor the second method, which is a lot quicker. You simply place a number in the draft where the revision will go. Place the same number next to the revision that is on the separate sheet of paper. When the paper is ready for typing, you or a typist can easily integrate the first draft and the revisions into the final typed paper.

Skill 60.   Type your paper neatly on good paper.

If at all possible, the final draft of your school papers should be typed. As a professor, I have had some students turn in hand-written papers. The students did this even though I explicitly stated that the papers must be typed. Teachers react negatively to handwritten papers because they are more time consuming and difficult to read than typed papers. If typed papers are a requirement, a handwritten paper will probably be penalized with a lower grade or turned back with a demand that it be typed.

Should you type the paper yourself or have it typed? Unless you are a good typist, I recommend that you have the paper prepared by a professional typist. He or she might charge you 6 to 10 dollars for a 10-page paper, but the cost is well worth it.

The ideal situation is for you to learn to use a word processor. The cost of computers that have this capability is getting very cheap. Many high schools and colleges have them available for students to use. The great advantage of word processors is that they allow you to easily revise the paper and then, at the end, they produce a very clean typed copy.

Here are some points to keep in mind when typing your paper or having it typed:

1. Use good bond paper that has substance and a nice surface sheen. If "clothes make the man," then "good bond paper makes the paper."

2. Use a high-quality typewriter ribbon, preferably a carbon ribbon. There is no substitute for a good carbon ribbon. It creates a much sharper type image than even a high-quality silk or nylon ribbon.

3. Use a word processor or a self-correcting typewriter. These typing machines make very clean corrections of typographical errors (called "typo's"). If you use an old-style typewriter, typo's will need to be corrected with correcting liquid. This procedure is usually satisfactory if the correcting liquid is applied neatly.

4. Type the paper double space, unless the teacher specifies otherwise.

5. Use an appropriate typeface. Typefaces come in two sizes, and in many different styles. Avoid an exotic typeface unless the situation warrants. I suggest that you use a conventional typeface, for example, Roman Gothic. The two sizes of type are *pica* (large) and *elite*

(small). Either one is acceptable. However, if you wish your paper to look concise or are concerned about exceeding the page limit, use an elite typeface. If you want to make the paper look longer, use a pica typeface.

6. Proofread the paper carefully after it is typed. Even experienced typists make mistakes, like skipping a whole sentence in the final draft of the paper.

7. Make certain that you have your name, date, course number, and teacher's name typed on the cover page, or on the first page if there is no cover page.

8. Make an extra copy of your paper before handing in the original. Teachers occasionally do misplace school papers. If so, you may be placed in the difficult position of demonstrating that you wrote the paper and handed it in. To be safe, either have a carbon copy made while the paper is being typed, or make a photocopy. I also recommend that you hold onto the handwritten draft for a while.

References

William Strunk, Jr. and E. B. White. *The Elements of Style. Third Edition*. New York: Macmillan, 1979.

This is the bible of how to write well. It is only 85 pages, but it tells almost everything you need to know about grammar and writing style. Everyone I know who takes writing seriously has read it.

Joseph Gibaldi and Walter S. Achtert. *MLA Handbook*. New York: Modern Language Association, 1980.

This is a useful reference book when writing a research paper for a school assignment. For example, it provides information about using the library, quoting from books, using correct punctuation, preparing a bibliography, and typing the paper.

6

Taking Tests

Even though tests are of different types, the skills required to prepare for them are similar. So are the skills needed while taking the test. Thus, I do not distinguish between weekly quizzes, midterm tests, final exams, mastery tests, etc. in this chapter.

Getting ready for tests is one of the most important tasks a student faces. For many students it is also one of the most unpleasant tasks.

Why is test taking so often unpleasant? There are two reasons. First, tests threaten you personally. It is anxiety provoking to realize that you may get a low score on a test and then you may feel like a failure, at least for a short while. Interestingly, if the threat factor is removed, most students enjoy being tested. For example, some educational games for children and adults consist of multiple-choice questions. The person responds by pressing the button that corresponds to his choice. A device will light up or a bell will go off to indicate whether the response is correct. These games are enjoyable because they are challenging and yet there are no negative consequences for poor performance. In contrast, a bad grade on a test can result in a student being placed on probation, excluded from school sports, or denied admission to college.

The other reason why tests are unpleasant is that they are often difficult. Think about it — you take a course to acquire *new* knowledge and skills. Even with lots of study, you may not feel completely in control of this new subject matter. The exam covers new content that you are still trying to master. That makes test taking difficult. Even if you know your subject matter well, the test situation requires you to reproduce it under pressure.

I do not claim that the proper use of study skills will turn test taking into a fun experience. Instead, my purpose in this chapter is to demonstrate how certain skills can lessen the trauma of test taking, and help you perform at your best. Using the skills will give you control over the test-taking situation.

Teachers test students in a variety of formats. They give short daily or weekly *quizzes* to evaluate a small amount of course content; *tests* to evaluate learning over a period of weeks and months; and *exams* that cover everything taught in the course. Many testing variations also occur. For example, a teacher may use a series of mastery tests that cover different parts of the course content. When a student feels that she knows a certain part of the content, she can take a mastery test on that part. If the student passes the mastery test at a specified level, she can proceed to the next part of the course. Otherwise the student re-studies the unmastered content and takes another version of the mastery test. The process of recycling is repeated until the student achieves mastery.

Another variation in testing is the take-home exam. Instead of a test in class, the teacher hands out the exam in class with instructions that it be completed and handed in by a certain date (usually several days to a week after being distributed).

You will also have to take tests that are not associated with courses. The most important of these tests are the aptitude tests required for admission to college and graduate school. Application to graduate work in business, law, medicine, engineering, the humanities, and science usually requires a test score on a specialized aptitude test.

The majority of tests are graded "on the curve." By this I mean that teachers grade students relative to each other. If a teacher grades strictly on the curve, she might give an A to the top 10 percent of the students; a B to the next 20 percent of the students; a C to another 40 percent; a D to the next 20 percent; and a grade of F to the lowest-scoring 10 percent of students.

There has been some grade inflation in recent years, meaning that teachers give a larger proportion of A's and B's on tests than they used to in the past. Traditionally only the top 10 to 15 percent of students received A's. This was customary practice at

Harvard and Berkeley when I was a student. Today it is not unusual for some teachers to award an A to between 30 and 50 percent of the students in a course.

If your teacher grades tests on a curve, you need to develop some idea of how other students in a course are doing. Frankly, this is easier said than done. How do you find out how your classmates are doing? The best technique I can think of is to analyze carefully your performance on the *first* test or quiz given by the teacher in a course. I remember the first seminars that I took in my doctoral program at Berkeley. I had no idea how good I was relative to my fellow classmates, although I knew they had to be exceptionally capable to have been admitted into the program. The first test that the professor gave was a midterm test covering half the textbook and the topics presented in the seminar up to that point. I studied hard, but received a "C" on the midterm. At that point I discovered just how good the other students in the seminar were.

I then made an appointment with the professor to find out what the "A" students had done that I had not done. It turned out that I was not memorizing enough of the details of the experiments described in the textbook. Thus I could not discuss these experiments in sufficient depth on the test. Some of my classmates apparently were devoting more effort to detailed study of the textbook than I was. I changed my study strategy accordingly and received an A on the final exam.

The only problem with this technique is that the first test may not be representative of what is to come later in the course. Or the teacher may only give one test, which is the final exam. If this is the case, you should try talking to some other students about the course. How hard are they studying? Which aspects of the content are they emphasizing? How much do they appear to know? If you can get answers to these questions, you will have a rough idea of how much effort you should spend in studying for a specific test.

The skills involved in active participation in class, reading assigned textbooks, and studying for a test are interrelated. Thus do not be surprised if you see an overlap between this chapter and the preceding chapters. The main idea that links the chapters is that if you wish to succeed in school, you must become an *active* learner. You cannot just let your eyes run over the textbook or let your ears absorb the teacher's lecture. You need to get actively involved with the course content. In this chapter I will show you how to use your time actively to prepare for tests and take them. Your goal is to get control over tests, rather than let tests control you and make your life miserable.

Before the Test

Skill 61. Learn your test schedule early in the term, and plan accordingly.

Taking tests is like going into an athletic contest. Once the contest starts, there is no time to plan a strategy. The strategy needs to be prepared beforehand. Preparation for tests involves finding out how many will be given, what type, when, and the standards of performance.

Consider the case of final exams. Most colleges and universities reserve the last week of the term entirely for exams. Many high schools also reserve several days for final testing. The schedule of exams during this week is usually printed in a publication called *Schedule of Classes* at the beginning of the term. You should work out your exam schedule early in the term. If luck is with you, you will have half a day or more between exams. These intervals between exams are important because they allow for rest and last-minute review. If luck is against you, you can find yourself with several back-to-back exams. You may spend two or three hours taking one exam, then have to rush to the next one.

When you learn your exam schedule, you can plan your preparation strategy accordingly. I recommend that you keep the entire exam week free for study and last-minute review. If possible, you should keep the preceding week free, too. When I was attending Harvard, this preceding week was known as "dead week," since no classes were held then. Students were expected to spend all of their time completing projects and preparing for exams. Obviously, you should be finished with term papers, projects, and personal business by the time final exams loom on the horizon. Otherwise your test anxiety can go through the ceiling as you try to juggle exam preparation and other tasks. The best way to stay calm during exam time is to limit the number of things you need to do.

The need to identify your final exam schedule and to plan your time around it also applies to midterm tests and to quizzes. The teacher should tell you the first week of the term the exact date on which each of these tests and quizzes is to occur. If not, be sure to ask the teacher for this information. Write these dates in your appointment book (see Skill 13), and then make sure you reserve some time prior to each test for study and review.

Skill 62. Control test anxiety by exercise, controlled breathing, deep muscle relaxation, positive thinking, meditation, and overpreparation.

If you get panicky and anxious as test time approaches, you are not alone. Many students experience lightheadedness, rapid heartbeat, and knots in their stomach the night before an important test. These physical symptoms of anxiety may not go away until the test has been written and handed in to the teacher. In fact, test anxiety is so common that it has been the subject of much research by psychologists.

Researchers have found that many students experience severe test anxiety, and that highly anxious students tend to score lower on tests than less anxious students. Test anxiety is usually situation-specific, which means that a student may be calm in other situations but freeze up when confronted with a test. Researchers have also found that anxiety is not always harmful. Up to a certain point, anxiety can improve performance. If you are too calm, you will not be motivated to do your best work. A moderate amount of anxiety produces a heightened state of alertness and concentration. However, if your anxiety reaches a high level, it can distract and disorient you so that you are "frozen" into inaction.

If you are anxious about taking tests, it is helpful to realize that this is a normal reaction. Next, you need to use techniques to control your anxiety. What are they? The following is a list of effective anxiety-reduction techniques. I have used all of them at one time or another.

1. *Exercise.* Rather than sit around and worry, engage in rigorous physical exercise. Physical activity will help you burn off nervous energy, maintain mental alertness, and stay healthy so that you can resist the stress of test taking. There is truth to the old saying, "A sound mind in a sound body."

Jogging is a recommended form of exercise to help one stay fit and mentally calm. I usually jog at least three times a week for ten to twenty minutes; this is sufficient to produce noticeable benefits. I know others who jog much more than this (15 to 30 miles a week), and this is fine, too. For those who dislike jogging, swimming is a good alternative.

I also recommend competitive sports. As a student at Harvard and Berkeley, I used to play a lot of tennis and squash. Now my favorite sport is racquetball because it provides a tremendous amount of exercise in a short period of time. A major benefit of racquetball and other competitive sports is that they require total concentration. It is difficult to worry about tests or other problems while you are tracking down a hard-hit ball. This relief from your problems makes it easier to cope with them when you finish playing.

Physical activity is an effective deterrent to test anxiety, used properly. The main precaution is that you need to *slowly* increase the intensity and length of the activity. You should not wait until you get test jitters before deciding to take up a rigorous sport. You are likely to exhaust or injure yourself. I recall that it took me almost six months before I could jog a mile comfortably. But since attaining that goal, I have been able to rely on jogging to help me stay calm in high-pressure situations.

2. *Controlled breathing.* A very good way to handle momentary feelings of anxiety is to monitor your breathing. As you become anxious, you tend to take short, shallow breaths. You can break this response pattern by taking a deep, slow breath. All you do is take in a deep breath, then let it out slowly and smoothly. After waiting a minute or two, you can repeat the steps if you wish. The only caution is that you should not breathe and exhale too forcefully and you should pause between each deep breath. Otherwise you run the risk of hyperventilating, which produces a lightheaded, dizzy feeling.

The Lamaze method, which is widely used in natural childbirth, relies heavily on controlled breathing to keep pain down to a tolerable level. The expectant mother is taught to take deep, regular breaths at a certain stage in labor, with the husband serving as "coach" to help her pace her breathing. The Lamaze method is very effective. Women trained in this method have much less need of anesthetics during childbirth than women who have not been trained.

The use of slow, deep breaths is very effective during critical periods of exam stress. Like most students, you may feel most anxious as you try to go to sleep the night before an important test, as you are about to leave your residence for the exam room, as you wait for the test to begin, and when you find that time is running short but you still have a substantial number of test items to answer. Try to get your breathing under control in these situations by taking slow, deep breaths.

3. *Deep muscle relaxation.* This is a good method for reducing tension and anxiety. The basic technique is to get in a comfortable position, then systematically tense and relax each muscle group in your body, from foot muscles to facial muscles. Some medical clinics and psychologists in private practice offer training in this method. However, you can learn deep muscle relaxation by obtaining a prerecorded audiotape in which an instructor directs you through the complete routine in tensing and relaxing each muscle group.

4. *Positive thinking.* The methods for controlling test anxiety described above focus on directly altering physiological functions of the body. Other methods are cognitive in nature. One of

these methods — positive thinking — is universally recommended. The essence of the method is to think positive thoughts when you feel test anxiety. The bad thing about anxiety is that it can drag you into the pits with negative thoughts like: "I'm going to fail"; "I'm going to freeze up in the exam room"; "I'll never get ready in time"; "I don't know this stuff"; and so on. Most students have experienced this type of negative thinking. You can cancel these negative thoughts by thinking positive thoughts: "I'm going to do just fine on this exam"; "I'm going to stay as cool as a cucumber in the exam room"; "I'm not ready now, but I'm going to just keep working and I'll be ready by exam time"; "I've really learned a lot so far in this course."

Positive thinking works well if you are not too anxious and if you are not unrealistic. It gives you a psychological boost. Like most other techniques, positive thinking must be practiced if it is to be effective. If you practice positive thinking over time, it will become a habit that you can call into play in stressful situations.

5. *Meditation.* Many students claim that meditation is very useful for helping them stay calm in stressful situations like tests.

A meditation technique that I have tried is to clear my head of all thoughts. An important element of this technique is to avoid getting upset if you find yourself thinking about something after you presumably cleared your head. Just calmly let the thought pass until your head is clear again. If instead you get upset, you just make it harder to control your anxious thoughts.

Several forms of meditation require you to channel your mental energy into a single focus. For example, you might look steadily at an object in the room. Another variation is to repeat a designated phrase, called a mantra. Some colleges and universities now offer courses in meditation, either by itself or in conjunction with yoga.

6. *Overpreparation.* Probably the best way to prevent test anxiety is to overprepare for the test. You just keep studying and studying until you feel that you know your subject inside out. This technique works because the better you know your subject, the more confident you will be about taking the test. Confidence is good prevention against anxiety.

To make this technique work, you need to allow a substantial amount of time for test study. Rather than reviewing each point in the text once or twice, review it three, four, or five times — until you can see the pages of the text in your mind's eye. Time-consuming, yes, but it is a real confidence booster and anxiety eliminator.

The worst test that I ever studied for occurred in my doctoral program. We had to take and pass an exam (called the "prelim") in order to continue on to the next phase of the program. The prelim tested our mastery of a huge reading list of books and journal articles in the various disciplines of psychology. All of us panicked over this exam because failure meant we were out of the program. Our time and financial investment would be down the drain.

The prelim was given just once a year, so many months of preparation were required for a one-shot performance. Some of my classmates did not cope very well at all. They avoided thinking about the prelim or they worried a lot without doing much study. I worried, too, but I also spent large amounts of time on study. I overprepared to the point that I developed photographic recall of key pages in the assigned readings. Even when I thought I knew a particular book chapter or journal article well, I kept reviewing it until I had totally mastered it.

Overpreparation worked. It kept my anxiety level down, and I passed the exam.

All the above techniquest have been used successfully to reduce anxiety. Which of these six techniques is best for controlling test anxiety? I do not think it is possible to rank them in order of effectiveness. You need to try each of them until you find those that work for you. Personally I think each technique has some value. For example, controlled breathing is good for reducing sudden attacks of anxiety, whereas overpreparation benefits you over a longer period of time.

Perhaps these techniques will also suggest other ways to keep your anxiety manageable. Over time, you will probably find yourself using techniques like these because you enjoy them, not merely to reduce test anxiety.

Skill 63. Identify the teacher's testing habits.

Like most people, teachers are creatures of habit. Being a teacher, I know that it is bothersome and time consuming to develop test items and scoring criteria, and to have the test typed and proofread. Therefore, I usually maintain the same test format each time I teach a particular course. I will write some new items and retain others from previous tests. The organization and types of items (e.g., multiple-choice, short answer) are usually not altered. My procedure for constructing tests is probably typical of what other teachers do.

Obviously, you can prepare for a test much easier if you have available copies of previous tests given by the teacher. The tests will tell you whether the teacher prefers multiple-choice items or essays; whether the teacher is a stickler for detail or is more interested in big ideas; and which parts of the textbook are most likely to be tested. There is nothing unethical about obtaining such tests, unless it is done illegally. In fact, some colleges and universities maintain a file of previously administered tests, so that all students have equal access to them.

Suppose a teacher is teaching a particular course for the first time. No previous tests are available to guide you. I think you can still benefit by examining tests that the teacher has given in *other* courses. This is because teachers tend to be consistent across the courses they are responsible for teaching.

Identifying the teacher's testing habits is a powerful technique. It can cut your test preparation by a third or more, because you can channel your efforts to those aspects of course content that are most likely to be tested.

Skill 64. Ask yourself questions that you think the teacher is likely to ask.

This is the most important skill that I will present in this chapter. Used properly, it will convert you from a passive learner into an active learner.

I also described this skill in the chapter on textbook study. I suggested that you ask yourself questions about each section of assigned textbook chapters. If you write down these questions, as I recommend you do, you can test yourself on them as you prepare for an exam. It is much more effective to answer these questions than to aimlessly scan the textbook pages in an attempt to review everything before the exam.

The more you learn, the better the questions you can generate. Therefore, even though you generated questions during your initial reading of the assigned material, I recommend that you generate a new set of questions as part of your final preparation for a test. The way to do this is to ask yourself, "What is the teacher most likely to ask on the test?" In other words, try to second-guess the teacher. You may enjoy seeing how many of the actual test questions you can anticipate.

When I was a student, I used this test preparation procedure with very good results. I was usually able to predict 50 to 75 percent of the teacher's questions, and thus could answer them easily on the test. This left me more time to think about the questions that I had not anticipated.

The essence of this skill is to get yourself into the mind-set of the teacher. After sitting through the teacher's classes, you should have developed a sense of his or her priorities, values, and interests. Use this knowledge to think through the types of questions that he or she would most likely ask on a test. For example, if the teacher stressed theory in his lectures, be sure to ask yourself questions about the theory presented in the assigned readings.

Students sometimes wonder whether they should write out answers to their self-generated questions. I personally think it is important to write down the questions, so that you can test yourself on them several times. However, I would not spend time writing detailed answers. I only write down a few key words; page numbers where the answers can be found in the text; or in the case of essay-type questions, very brief outlines. If you write down detailed answers, you are likely to just read them and the accompanying questions without really testing yourself.

You cannot devote equal attention to everything covered in a course. There simply is too much knowledge available in most areas of study. Thus, you need to become selective in what you try to remember and think about. A test represents the teacher's conception of what is worth remembering and reflecting on. Since you must take the teacher's test — rather than one of your own design — you need to anticipate what the teacher will select as most worth knowing.

Skill 65. Analyze the types of items likely to be on the test.

There are three major types of learning outcomes in a school or college course, each tested in a different way:

1. Recall of information. Teachers usually test your ability to recall information by asking multiple-choice questions, matching questions, and short-answer questions.
2. Ability to think, that is, to compare, analyze, synthesize, predict, or evaluate. This ability is usually tested by essay questions.
3. Ability to apply skills. Skills are tested by having the student solve problems that require the application of the skills.

You need to anticipate which of these learning outcomes the teacher is most interested in. The test may be predominantly of one type or a mix of several types.

Each type of learning outcome requires a different method of test preparation. If you think that the teacher will be testing for information recall, ask yourself, "What are the facts that are most likely to be tested on the exam?" Then generate a question for each fact or set of facts that you think the teacher might expect you to have memorized.

Suppose your hunch is that the teacher will test your ability to think and communicate. Now test preparation is more complicated. It is impossible to generate and answer every essay question that could be asked about every topic covered in the course. Therefore, I recommend that you generate four or five thought-provoking essay questions, each of which covers a different range of course topics. Next outline answers to all of them. Finally, write an actual essay response, under timed conditions, to one of them; this will give you practice in writing an exam-type essay. This total process should only take a few hours of your time. I found it quite worthwhile when I was a student at Harvard, where most exams required essay responses.

Even though you may not anticipate the actual essay questions, the process of generating and answering your own questions requires you to think about the major concepts covered in the course. The teacher may test these concepts in a different way on the exam, but they are likely to be the same concepts.

Some tests require you to demonstrate a skill. For example, you may be asked to demonstrate the correct procedure for lighting a bunsen burner, for solving a quadratic equation, or for treading water. Obviously you should practice these skills before the test. Also try drawing a flow chart (similar to a time line; see Skill 30), with each step of the process written in. This is an excellent way to learn a skill involving a specific pattern of behavior. Drawing a flow chart is also an ideal way to demonstrate the skill on a written exam.

If the skill to be tested involves problem solving, a different preparation strategy is required. You cannot anticipate all the specific problems that the teacher might give you on a test. However, you can anticipate the *types* of problems that will be on the test. Once you have done this, you should practice solving a number of problems of each type until you feel comfortable with them.

Most students are not trained to think in the way described above. Their view of learning is simple; they call everything "knowledge." When you think about it, though, you realize that there are different types of "knowledge" — facts, organized sets of facts, ideas, motor skills, and problem-solving skills. Even values and attitudes are a type of "knowledge" that can be taught. Once you are aware of the different learning outcomes, you can plan your study strategy to match the particular learning outcomes that will be tested on the exam. The result will be more efficient test study and better grades.

Skill 66.   Balance your textbook review between quizzing yourself, reviewing notes, and scanning the text.

The task of preparing for tests can be overwhelming. One of the most difficult problems you will face is deciding how to review several hundred pages of a textbook that you know are fair game for the teacher's test. There is a temptation to try to re-read every page so that you will not miss any piece of information that might appear on a test item.

I do not think that this strategy is practical. What I recommend instead is to spend most of your time making up questions about the text and answering them (see Skills 25 and 64). Also, if you have taken notes on the textbook, spend some time reviewing them. Finally, I suggest you scan — not read — the textbook. The purpose of scanning is to check that significant items of information were not overlooked in your previous study. This three-step strategy of self-quizzing, note reviewing, and scanning is much more efficient than trying to read or re-read the entire text.

Skill 67.   Memorize rather than use crib sheets.

You may have heard of students who write key formulas, dates, names, and other information on small pieces of paper (called "crib sheets"). The students take crib sheets into the exam room concealed under their sleeves or somewhere else. Of course, this practice is unethical. If a student is caught by the teacher or by other students, he or she is in for a severe penalty.

What alternative do you have? I recommend that you go ahead and make a few crib sheets on essential concepts that will be tested. Then *memorize* your crib sheets, since you cannot take them into the exam. Memorizing takes time, but it can be done.

There are several ways to improve your memory. The way I recommend is to make an association between what you need to remember and something else. For example, suppose you need to remember the capitols of all the European nations. You can make up an easy-to-remember phrase for each nation: Italians like to *r*un (Rome). Belgians are very *b*usy (Brussels). Spaniards are *m*oviegoers (Madrid), and so on.

Lists can be remembered more easily by making up a sentence that uses the first letter of each item on the list. Suppose you want to remember the names of five major civil war battles and the order in which they occurred. Suppose the five battles are: Battle of Shiloh, Battle of the Seven Days, Battle of Antietam, Battle of Gettysburg, and Battle of the Wilderness. Here is a sentence that could help you remember this list: Save some days in August to go waterskiing. The words in the sentence cue the battles this way: Save (Shiloh) some days (Seven Days) in August (Antietam) to go (Gettysburg) waterskiing (Wilderness).

The most important aid to memory, of course, is practice. Keep practicing your recall of essential information that you think will be tested.

Skill 68.   Form a study group to prepare for a test.

I only started using this technique when I was in graduate school. However, I wish I had made use of it previously in college and high school.

When students passed the prelim exam at Berkeley (see Skill 62), the next step was to start studying for "orals." In the oral exam, a committee of four professors asks the student questions about any aspect of psychology that they wish. I studied for this exam with a group of other doctoral students. We met once a week and quizzed each other. It was a great way to prepare because each of us got a lot of practice generating questions and answering them. Even when it was not our turn, we learned by listening to others' questions and answers.

You may not want to use this technique to prepare for quizzes, but give it a try when studying for important midterm tests and final exams. The technique will work even if you can find only one other classmate to work with. Even one study session can help you greatly in getting ready for a test.

Skill 69. Plan for the supplies you will need for the test.

The less you have to worry about before the test, the better. If you have laid out the supplies you will need beforehand, you can pick them up and go calmly to the test location. Otherwise you may get into a mad scramble trying to remember what items you need and tracking them down. The most commonly needed items are: paper, at least two pencils with erasers or two pens, ruler, calculator, stapler, and something to munch on.

Most of the items are obvious, but why the stapler? You may need to write your answer on several sheets of paper, and it is easy for them to get separated when the teacher collects your test. If you bring a small stapler with you, you can staple your test together. This procedure securely holds the pages together and is much neater-appearing than a creased set of pages.

I recommend that you collect your supplies the day before the test. Then, on test day, you have one less thing to worry about.

On the Day of the Test

Skill 70. Get to the testing room well in advance.

The time and location of tests are not usually a problem in junior high or high school. Tests are scheduled in the same room and at the same time that the class regularly meets. However, you are likely to encounter a different situation when you take aptitude tests (for example, the Scholastic Aptitude Test) and college exams. The midterm and final exam for a course may be scheduled at a different time and in a different room than the regular meetings of the course.

By all means double-check the time and place of the test well beforehand. I have known students who showed up for tests at the wrong room or wrong time. If you are not familiar with the exam room, determine its location in advance. Colleges and universities often have buildings with odd layouts and odd room-numbering systems.

Skill 71.   *Try to get a comfortable seat near the test administrator.*

It sometimes makes a difference where you sit in the exam room. For example, if there is a lot of noise outdoors, you will want to avoid sitting near windows. It is difficult to answer test questions to the accompaniment of lawnmowers. The exam room may be located off a noisy corridor, in which case you will want to sit away from the door. And then there is the problem of noisy students. I personally get distracted by students who cough, wheeze, or mutter a lot, or who have the habit of shuffling their feet or tapping their pencil. My experience has been that students who jerk about or look nervous before the test are the ones most likely to be distracting during the test.

If the test is being held in a large lecture hall or auditorium, it is important to sit near the front of the room. You can hear the test administrator's directions more clearly, and it is easier to get the administrator's attention if you have questions to ask. I used to administer various aptitude tests (for example, the Scholastic Aptitude Test and the Graduate Record Examination) to earn extra money when I was in graduate school. These tests were administered to hundreds of students at one sitting. The students who sat furthest from me were the ones most likely not to hear directions. While I was answering their questions one by one, the others had already started the test and thus had an advantage.

Skill 72.   Read test directions carefully.

Most of us do not follow directions very well. Perhaps we do not want anyone telling us what to do, or we think that we can figure out what to do ourselves. Students often think that reading directions carefully takes too much time. They are too eager to get on with the task of answering test items.

Serious mistakes can be made on tests where answers must be recorded on a separate answer sheet by making a pencil mark within the correct brackets. Because these tests are machine-scored, you must follow the exact directions. If you put your marks in the wrong set of columns, your answers will be scored wrong by the test-scoring machine. It has no way to determine that you knew the correct answer, but followed the test directions incorrectly.

You should be on the lookout for statements like "Answer 3 questions from the following choice of 5 questions." As a professor, I have seen quite a few students overlook this direction and try to answer all five questions. Because of time pressure, the students' answers are not likely to be as good as if they had followed the directions and just answered three questions. A similar error is to answer three questions, but from the wrong set of five.

Directions for multiple-choice questions and the items themselves should be read carefully. Multiple-choice items usually have one correct answer, but sometimes the item is written so that more than one answer is correct. These items are usually introduced by a question like "Which of these statements is (are) true?" Assuming that this is a standard item with 4 choices, the question — "Which of these statements is (are) true?" — indicates that one, two, three, or all four of the choices may be correct.

A common type of direction for multiple-choice items is a note concerning penalties for guessing. Teachers sometimes subtract a point or fraction of point for each incorrectly answered item. If this is the case, you need to know about it. If you are so unsure about the correct answer to a multiple-choice item that you can only guess, it may be to your advantage not to answer it at all.

If the test specifies point values for different items, these should be read carefully. A test may have a lot of items (usually multiple-choice) that do not count much toward your grade. Another section of the test may only have a few essay items, with the directions indicating that they will count heavily toward your grade. Obviously you should read the directions carefully to figure out how much effort you should spend on each item.

Skill 73.   Plan how much time to spend on each section of the test.

There are two types of tests — timed and untimed. If you are taking an untimed test, it is not important how you allocate your time. You can take as much time as you need to complete the test. A timed test requires a different approach. You need to plan a strategy that ensures you will finish the test within the time limit.

First, make certain that you have an accurate watch. Your classroom may not have a clock. If there is a clock, it may not be accurate. Your best bet is to bring your own watch to the exam room. It should be a watch on which minutes are clearly indicated.

After reading the test directions, spend a few minutes deciding how much time to spend on each section of the test. Some students, however, are reluctant to do this. They think their time is better spent by answering test items right away. The problem with this strategy is that the students may get stuck on a particular test item, or write a very long answer. Then they find out that they cannot finish the test within the allotted time.

If the test is one long set of test items, I recommend grouping them into sets. For example, if I have 90 minutes to answer 100 items, I might group the items into five sets of 20 items each. Allowing 5 minutes for initial planning and 5 minutes for last-minute checking leaves me 80 minutes for answering the items. I would divide 5 into 80 minutes, which is 16 minutes. This means I should try to complete each set of 20 items in 16 minutes.

When I have figured the amount of time to spend on a particular test section, I write it in the margin next to that section. I also write down the actual clock time by which I should have completed each section. Using the above example, let's assume the test starts at 11:00 and I finish initial planning by 11:05. This means I should complete the first set of 20 items by 11:21, the second set by 11:37, and so forth. I write these times next to the item that marks the end of each set. Now, in working through the test, I have a good idea of whether I am working at a good pace. If I do not complete a set by my estimated deadline, I know it will be necessary to speed up on the next set. If I beat the deadline, I know that I can spend more time on the next set, or more time checking my answers after completing all items.

Skill 74.   Answer easy test items first to build confidence and momentum.

One test-taking strategy is to answer the items in the order that they appear on the test. Another strategy is to answer the easy items right away, leaving the more difficult items until later. Is this second strategy better?

I think it is. When I was faced with a difficult exam at Harvard and Berkeley, I usually answered the easiest items first — the ones that I was sure I could answer correctly. This procedure built my confidence. More importantly, it gave me a sense of accomplishment.

I marked each item on the exam that I needed to return to later. After completing the easy items, I started working on the more difficult items. If an item was especially difficult, I delayed answering it again. Finally, after responding to the medium-difficulty items, I tackled the most difficult items. This strategy is effective because it ensures that you tackle every item and that you give your best test performance. Nothing is more discouraging than to find out there were items at the end of a test that you could have answered correctly, but were not able to because you ran out of time.

Skill 75.   *Take mini-breaks during the test.*

You may find that you do better on a test by taking short breaks than by working continuously. The reason is that short rest breaks restore your energy, whereas continuous work gradually reduces your efficiency.

Most tests are tightly scheduled, so you do not have much time for breaks. However, even brief breaks of 10 to 15 seconds can give you an energy boost. Some students close their eyes or rest their heads on the table. Another idea is to bring a moist towelette (the type that comes in a sealed packet) to the exam room. Wiping your face and hands with a towelette is refreshing, yet it only takes a few seconds of your time.

During your break, try using one of the techniques presented in Skill 62 for controlling test anxiety. Any of the techniques of controlled breathing, deep muscle relaxation, positive thinking, or meditation can be done unobtrusively while you remain seated.

In addition to taking brief breaks from the test, I recommend that you bring your favorite food to the test room if permitted. Foods like raisins, peanuts, and trail mix will help to maintain your energy level through the test.

Skill 76.   *Write an exam esssay the same way you would a course paper.*

The procedure for writing an exam essay is the same as that for writing school papers (see Chapter 5), except for three differences. The time factor in the two situations is obviously different: you usually have 30 minutes or less to write an exam essay, whereas you may have weeks to write a school paper. Second, you cannot ask anyone for feedback while you are writing an exam essay. And third, the opportunity for revising an exam essay is very limited.

Because time for exam essays is so limited, there is a tendency to start writing immediately to be sure that you get some words on paper. It is better, though, to take several minutes to plan your essay response. Brainstorming and outlining are especially important. Make a note of everything you want to say before writing your answer. The reason for this advice is that your first draft will probably be your final draft, except for a few revisions that can be made quickly.

My experience as a professor indicates that professors in general are less concerned about matters of style in exam essays than in course papers. They know that you are under pressure in writing an exam and do not have the time to refine your writing style. But professors do hold you responsible for *what* you say. That is why outlining and brainstorming are so important. You want to make certain that you get all your ideas down on paper, even though they may not be expressed elegantly.

Another factor that affects teachers' judgment of your exam essays is organization. You may be penalized if it appears that you have put down ideas and references that are out of order or irrelevant to the essay topic. A good technique is to write an introductory paragraph that explains how your essay is organized.

You should read the exam directions carefully to be sure that an essay-type response is required. For example, I sometimes write exam questions of this type, "List the five steps in ..." or "Describe briefly the three major ..." No comparisons, analysis, or evaluation is called for in these questions. Yet some of my students will write an organized essay response well beyond what I require for a perfect score. The word "list" means just that — a set of numbered descriptions. Writing an essay, when brief phrases will do, takes a lot of valuable time and is not likely to improve your exam grade.

Skill 77. *In writing exam essays, leave blank spaces for revisions.*

You will not have time to make extensive revisions in your exam essays. However, you may have some time to rewrite a few sentences, improve transitions between paragraphs, or even rewrite an entire paragraph. As a student, I made sure to write my answers on wide-ruled paper so that I could write in minor changes right above the place in the essay where they belonged.

I also left a few inches at the top of each page. If I made a major change, such as rewriting a complete sentence or paragraph, I would write it there. Then I would draw an arrow from this new version to the place in the essay where it was to be inserted. This simple technique makes for a neat-appearing exam essay, yet it allows you the freedom to make revisions. If you do not use the extra space, the exam pages still look neat.

Some students write each of their revisions at the end of their first essay draft. Then they number each revision, and also place that number at the place in the essay where it belongs. In effect, this is a system of footnotes. I do not like this procedure because it requires the teacher to go back and forth from the first draft to the page or pages on which the revisions appear. In the procedure described above, everything the teacher needs to read in the essay is on the same page.

Skill 78. *When uncertain of the correct answer to a test item, make a reasonable guess.*

Guessing is an important part of the test-taking process. Even very bright students guess when they are not certain of the answer to a test item. If done intelligently, guessing is a good strategy.

Consider the case of multiple-choice items. If the teacher will not penalize you for incorrect answers, it is to your advantage to answer every item, even if you have to guess. For example, a typical multiple-choice item has four options, one of which is correct. Therefore, even if you know nothing about the item content, you would have one chance in four of selecting the correct answer just by guessing. If you can eliminate one of the options as being definitely incorrect, you can improve your chances even more. For example, if you can eliminate two of the options, and then pick one of the two remaining options by chance, you would have one chance in two of guessing the correct answer.

The decision to guess becomes complicated when there is a penalty for incorrect guesses. If the penalty is small — for example, deduction of a quarter-point for each incorrect answer — you should seriously consider guessing. The advantage of guessing increases if you can eliminate one or two of the options as incorrect, or if you sense that a particular choice is probably right. If the penalty is more severe, then I would not recommend guessing the answer to any item about which I knew nothing. I would only consider guessing if I could narrow down to two choices, and one of them appeared more probably correct than another.

Guessing on exam essays is another matter. I have a simple recommendation to make: do not guess. As a teacher, I occasionally read exams where the student has written answers to essay questions they knew nothing about. They write down anything they know in the distant hope that they will stumble onto the correct answer. They almost never hit the mark, and so their answers create a poor impression. If you do not know anything about the topic being tested by the essay question, just skip it. It is better to skip over the question than to write a meaningless response.

If you know something about the topic, but cannot remember a specific fact, such as someone's name or a date, I recommend you leave it out of your exam essay. If you guess wrong, the teacher will probably take points from your score. However, if you just do not refer to the fact, the teacher may ignore it. Also, sometimes you can substitute a more general fact for the specific fact that you are unable to recall. For example, if you cannot remember the specific year of a historic battle, but you know it occurred in the sixteenth century, that piece of information will probably be acceptable to the teacher.

Skill 79. Double-check that you have answered all test items.

As a test draws to a close, I recommend that you quickly check the test to be certain that you have answered all of the items. Overlooking items can happen if you skip around a test, answering easy items first and more difficult items later. Also, the sheer stress of test taking may be sufficient to cause students to overlook test items and important directions.

As a student, I overlooked test items on a few occasions, and I know other students did, too. I recommend you double-check the test every time you take one.

Skill 80. Avoid becoming distracted by what other students do during the test.

There is a tendency to conform your test behavior to what other students do. This practice sometimes works against you. For example, as a professor, I generally give untimed tests. Some students hand in their completed tests much sooner than other students. Eventually a steady flow of students comes to the front of the room to turn in their tests. The dwindling number of students who remain working appear to become nervous as they see others turn in their tests. They are under no pressure from me to work fast, so they must be putting this pressure on themselves. Rather than judging their behavior by what others do, they should simply ignore other students and work at their own pace.

In taking a timed test, be careful to follow your own game plan. Once you have worked out your time estimates for completing different sections of the test, try to stick to this schedule. If you look around and see that some of your classmates are further along on the test than you, that should not cause you to change your strategy. Other students may be following a different strategy — or none at all!

Some students like to hand in their completed test well before the time limit. They think that they will impress the teacher by doing this. However, I have never known a teacher who cared or even remembered whether a particular student handed in a test early.

When I was a student, I almost always used all of the allotted time for a test. After finishing the test, I would use the extra time to check and double-check my answers. This procedure is very effective in tests involving mathematical computations. If you have extra time, do the computations a second time to make certain that you have not made any careless errors. If you are taking an essay exam, you can use the left-over time to revise your writing. Also, you can rewrite sections of an essay that have been heavily revised to make them more readable. In other words, use *all* of the time that the teacher allows. Do not be distracted by other students who choose to turn in their tests before the time limit is up.

References

James H. Divine and David W. Kylen. *How To Beat Test Anxiety and Score Higher on Your Exams.* Woodbury, New York: Barron's Educational Series, 1979.
    If you are bothered by test anxiety, this little book has many specific ideas to help you.

Michael Donner. *How To Beat the S.A.T. and All Standardized Multiple-Choice Tests.* New York: Workman Publishing, 1981.

This book focuses on the Scholastic Aptitude Test, which you usually must take when applying to college. The author gives you 17 rules to follow when taking this and related tests. Your local bookstore should have similar books that give you practice on answering the type of test items found in the S.A.T. and similar aptitude tests.

Concluding Note

Writing *Making the Grade* has given me new insights into the requirements—and rewards—of effective study. I hope your reading, and continued use, of this book will do the same for you.

How can you tell that your study efforts are paying off? Here are some of the benefits you can look forward to from using the skills in *Making the Grade*.

1. You will be able to study smarter, not harder.
2. You will be able to get started on challenging assignments sooner, and with more confidence.
3. Your grades and test scores will improve.
4. You will move toward the top of your class.
5. Your performance in school will assure you the opportunity to continue your education at a quality college or university.

Remember, learning effective study skills takes time. Most students continue to refine their study skills with each new course or assignment. For this reason, *Making the Grade* is designed for you to use as a reference manual for years to come.

Do not become discouraged if you find that it takes you a long time to master certain skills. Just take it one step at a time. Remember Skill 4, especially: Break a big task into small, manageable tasks. This will keep you going until you can see your progress. Every skill you acquire will contribute to your success—in school, and in life.

Index

Index